W9-CEC-020

Delinquency and Drift

Delinquency and

From the research program of the Center for the Study of Law and Society

NEW YORK · LONDON · SYDNEY

Theodore Lownik Library
Illinois Benedictine College
Lisle, Illinois 60532

Drift

David Matza

University of California, Berkeley

John Wiley & Sons, Inc.

HV
9069
·M37
c. 2

Copyright © 1964 by John Wiley & Sons, Inc.
All Rights Reserved
Reproduction or translation of any part of this work beyond
that permitted by Sections 107 or 108 of the 1976 United States
Copyright Act without the permission of the copyright owner
is unlawful. Requests for permission or further information
should be addressed to the Permissions Department, John
Wiley & Sons, Inc.

12 13 14 15 16 17 18 19 20

ISBN 0 471 57708 1
Library of Congress Catalog Card Number: 64-18135
Printed in the United States of America

To Cynthia, Naomi, and Karen

Preface

I N this book I have attempted to develop a conception of delinquency which differs in some ways from that projected in positive criminology. In revising the current conception, I have tried to fit many of the empirical observations of positive criminologists into a framework more consistent with classical assumptions and teachings. The main teaching of classical criminology was the insistence that the criminal be seen in a legal context. Consequently, I have stressed throughout the *connection* between delinquent thought and the ideas and practices that pervade contemporary juvenile law and its administration. This connection is expressed in the idea of neutralization, by which the legal bind is episodically subverted *on its own terms,* and a conception of subterranean support, by which agents of convention and law unwittingly and with good will contribute their services and sentiments to the feasibility of neutralization.

In developing a conception of the classic delinquent—a delinquent seen in legal context—I have been led quite naturally, or so I would like to believe, to a portrayal that incorporates the associated assumptions of classical criminology. Thus, I have tried to convey the sense in which the precepts featured in a subculture of delinquency are only marginally different from those apparent in common sentiments of American life; and I have attempted to utilize the classic conception of a will to crime in order to maintain the ineradicable element of choice and freedom inherent in the condition of delinquent drift.

DAVID MATZA

Berkeley, California
March 1964

Acknowledgments

THE number of debts one incurs in writing a book is surprisingly large. There are the family members who bear the heavy burden of oscillation between irritable depression and mindless immersion, the many colleagues and students who give freely of their time in criticizing the ideas that go into a manuscript, and the institutions which in a variety of ways expedite the observing, thinking, and writing that go into a book. It is a mark of the generosity of familial, collegial, academic, and granting institutions that in each case the author never really repays the debts he has incurred—he merely acknowledges them.

Many persons have commented on various portions of the manuscript at different stages of its development. Their comments have been intellectually helpful and emotionally supportive. Whenever possible I have responded to suggestions made by Melvin Tumin, Albert Cohen, James Short, Donald Cressey, William Petersen, Sheldon Messinger, Erving Goffman, Ruth Kornhauser, Philip Selznick, Aaron Cicourel, Edwin Lemert, Irving Piliavin, Jerome Skolnick, Carl Werthman, Sally Davis, and Marvin Scott. If some of those mentioned do not recognize what appears in this book, it is because I took their criticisms of an earlier manuscript so seriously as to write what I think is a fundamentally different book.

I wish also to thank the institutions that in many ways afforded me the time and supplied the facilities with which this book could be written. These institutions include the Law School at the University of Chicago and its Program for Behavioral Science and Law which was supported by the Ford Foundation and stimulated by Dean Levi, Francis Allen, Hans Zeisel, and others; the Center for the Study of Law and Society at the University of California, directed and guided by Philip Selznick and Sheldon Messinger, and the President's Committee on Youth Crime and Juvenile Delinquency whose financial support and initial encouragement led to the formation of a Curriculum Development Program in Crime and Delinquency. That program is one of the projects of the Center for the Study of Law and Society, and this book is one of a series of contributions that will emanate from it.

Finally, I should like to acknowledge my special debt to Gresham Sykes. Many of the ideas in this book were first developed in collaboration with him. If in this independent effort any additional contribution is made, he must receive a large share of the credit. If, however, my efforts have been misguided, I alone am responsible.

D.M.

Contents

[1]

The Positive Delinquent

E ACH of us carries in mind pictures of a variety of social statuses; among these is one of the juvenile delinquent. Our
basic conceptions of the juvenile delinquent, and those of other
contemporary figures, are imbedded in these pictures. Consequently, research frequently does not progress deeply enough to
offend and thus qualify our conceptions. Research typically is
guided by basic conceptions rather than being designed to question them.

Our picture of the delinquent consists of the basic assumptions
we make about him. Currently and for almost one hundred years
our assumptions about the delinquent have been those of the
positive school of criminology. My main purpose in this book is
to question and modify the positivist portrait. Since assumptions
are usually implicit, they tend to remain beyond the reach of
such intellectual correctives as argument, criticism, and scrutiny.
Thus, to render assumptions explicit is not only to propose a thesis;
more fundamentally it is to widen and deepen the area requiring
exploration. Assumptions implicit in conceptions are rarely inconsequential. Left unattended, they return to haunt us by shaping or
bending theories that purport to explain major social phenomena.
Assumptions may prompt us to notice or to ignore discrepancies
or patterns that may be observed in the empirical world. Conceptions structure our inquiry.

Moreover, pictures are intimately related to the explanation of
social systems. Systems of action may usually be typified in ideal
fashion. Indeed, this simplification is almost mandatory if the
analyst wishes to proceed to the task of explanation. A system,
whether it be capitalism or delinquency, has exemplars, basic
figures who perpetrate the system. The accurate characterizing of

1

exemplars is a crucial step in the development of explanatory theory. Given the present state of knowledge, pictures are not true or false, but rather plausible or implausible. They more or less remind us of the many discrete individuals who make up a social category. All conceptions of the delinquent bear some resemblance to some of the discrete individuals who are involved in delinquent enterprise. Currently, therefore, the test of a picture is its ring of truth. Which picture most consistently reminds those who are in intimate and persistent contact with the variety of delinquents of the real thing? My purpose in writing a book of this sort is that the pictures of delinquency that thus far have been drawn do not remind me and many others of the real things they purport to explain. It is not that they distort reality, for all pictures do that; rather, in distorting reality, current pictures seem to lose what is essential in the character of delinquent enterprise.

Systems of action have exemplars and a portrayal of them is a crucial step in the elaboration of causal theory. Thus, for example, a plausible picture of the capitalist was implicit in the various theories explaining the rise of capitalism. This hardly means that a system may be reduced to the character of exemplars; rather, an exemplar is a personification or microcosm of the system. A crucial step from a Marxian to a Weberian theory of the origins of capitalism consisted of a basic shift in the portrait of the exemplary capitalist. Somewhere in the dialectic between competing scholars the pirate capitalist of Marx was transformed to the bookkeeper capitalist of Weber. The more authentic ring of Weber's portrait is largely responsible for the more widespread acceptance of his rather than Marx's theory of the emergence of capitalism. Whatever the other virtues of Marx's theory, it suffers from an initial inplausibility. It seems conceived on a false note. How, we ask, can we believe in a theory that apparently falsifies the character of the exemplars? Whatever the failings of Weber's theory, it seems more plausible because it is more reminiscent of the early capitalists we have studied or read about.

Conceptions of the delinquent and a variety of theories explaining his emergence have appeared within the context of criminology. The nature of modern criminology—its connection with, but primarily its considerable insulation from, the rest of social science—has affected our deepest conceptions of the delinquent.

Criminology in recent years has become increasingly integrated into sociology, but it was and still is a separate field with its own traditions and preconceptions.[1] Modern criminology is the positive school of criminology. According to most scholars, it begins with the views of Lombroso, which consisted of a rather fundamental repudiation of the earlier classical viewpoint of Beccaria, Bentham, Carrara, and others. This fundamental shift, signaled by Lombroso and largely carried through by Ferri, laid the basic assumptions of criminological thought, and these assumptions persist to this day. Like Ferri, most of us are positivists in that we share the same conceptions of the nature of criminological inquiry and the character of the subject we explore—the criminal actor. The legacy of positive criminology consists of three fundamental assumptions. All are very much alive today, and each contributes to our basic conception of the delinquent. Each was a reaction to the assumptions of classical criminology. Each, I propose to argue, was an overreaction. The picture of the delinquent developed in this book is a revision of that positivist conception. My aim is to incorporate modified versions of the classical viewpoint into the framework of positive criminology.

The most celebrated and thus the most explicit assumption of positive criminology is the primacy of the criminal actor rather than the criminal law as the major point of departure in the construction of etiological theories. The explanation of crime, according to the positive school, may be found in the motivational and behavioral systems of criminals. Among these systems, the law and its administration is deemed secondary or irrelevant. This quest for explanation in the character and background of offenders has characterized all modern criminology, irrespective of the particular causal factors espoused.

The shift from the biological orientation of Lombroso to the social and psychological orientation of the modern criminologist has misled some as to the true influence of the Positive School of modern criminology. If this term "positivist" is applied to Sutherland, for example, someone will object that Sutherland's theory of behavior [leading to crime] is not the same as Lombroso's. The importance of the Positive School is that it focused attention on motivation and on the . . . criminal. This is true of every theory of criminal behavior which is discussed in textbooks today, even though the explanation is in terms of social and group factors rather than in terms of biological factors. The shift in criminological thinking has been from a biological to a sociological and psychological explanation of behavior, not in terms of a shift in interest from the criminal to crime. The emphasis is still on the . . . offender, not crime.[2]

A major consequence of the modern positivist approach has been to reverse the aphorism of Carrara, a classical criminolgist. Whereas Carrara suggested that crime was above all an infraction and not an action, the positivist suggests the very opposite. Delinquency, according to positivism, is best viewed as springing from life situations. It is action. The complex relationship between delinquents and legal institutions has received little attention. Contemporary social and psychological theories of delinquency unwittingly capitalize on the clarity and sharpness with which biological positivism broke with the classical stress on legal institutions. Biological theories of crime made a more reasonable claim than subsequent theories to the irrelevance of legal institutions. The relation between the vagaries of the human organism and the form taken by legal systems hardly seemed a worthwhile subject of inquiry. Legal institutions, however, are an important element of society, and by the very terms of sociological theory —the relation of man to society—their connection with crime warrants consideration. Modern sociological theories of delinquency stress the effects of social class, ethnic affiliation, family, and neighborhood. But we sociologists have continued to ignore the sense in which crime is a peculiar reaction to legal institutions, even though the ambitions of our discipline commit us to the exploration of man's relation to the full round of social institutions.

The delinquent stands in some relation to the legal order, its demands, principles, and doctrines. This relationship is his defining characteristic, and it would be surprising if the description of it in its complexity failed to clarify the motivational system of delinquents. Positive criminology has come very close to ignoring the defining character of delinquents—the fact that they commit infractions—in its various explanations of delinquency. Consequently, it has failed to scrutinize the nature of legal prohibitions and the emergence of delinquent customs which parallel and distort legal views.

The positive school . . . marks the beginning in the study of crime causation of emphasis on the nature of the criminal act per se. . . . The positive school represents the first formulations and applications to the field of criminology of the point of view, methodology, and logic of the natural sciences to the study of human behavior.[3]

Positivism, blessed with the virtues and prestige of science, has little concern for the essence of phenomenon it wishes to study. That is metaphysics. Thus, positive criminology could for close to a century display little concern for the essence of crime— infraction.

The second abiding feature of the positive school may be traced to its quest for scientific status. Positive criminology, at its inception and even now, contrasts its scientific view of man with that of classical philosophy. "Whereas the classical school accepted the doctrine of free will, the positive school based the study of criminal behavior on scientific determinism."[4] This it did and more. Positive criminology fashioned an image of man to suit a study of criminal behavior based on scientific determinism. It rejected the view that man exercised freedom, was possessed of reason, and was thus capable of choice. Man, endowed with freedom and reason, is held to be a conception that is "essentially pre-scientific in any modern sense of the human behavior sciences."[5]

To understand the positivist view of criminal action, it is necessary to distinguish between two kinds of determinism—hard and soft. All social science is, to one extent or another, deterministic. Modern sociology, however, has in considerable measure shed its early hard determinism. Modern criminology has not. The difference between hard and soft determinism is that one merely directs the analyst, whereas the other makes a fundamental contention regarding the nature of human action. Positive criminology broke with what it regarded an "animistic, self-determining, free will kind of thinking."[6] It substituted for the classical model an image of man as fundamentally constrained. Determinism for the positive school of criminology was not merely a heuristic principle; it was a vision that likened man to physical and chemical particles. Every event is caused. Human freedom is illusory. The positive school of criminology concurred with the dictum of Schopenhauer.

Every man, being what he is and placed in the circumstances which for the moment obtain, but which on their part also arise by strict necessity, can absolutely never do anything else than just what at that moment he does do. Accordingly, the whole course of a man's life, in all its incidents great and small, is as necessarily predetermined as the course of a clock.[7]

Positive criminology was from the outset greatly affected by the hard determinism of its early biological foundations. The early spokesmen of positive criminology, Lombroso and Ferri, hoped to combine social, geographical, and psychological factors with a biological base to explain and predict criminality. The assumptions of biological constraint—pathology hardly allows of will—were deemed equally applicable to social and psychological events. Furthermore, when the revolt against the hegemony of biology began, its hard determinism became part of the stance of the new disciplines. Like Hassan the fig vender, they were not to be outdone. Spencerian sociology, Watsonian behaviorism, Freudian psychic determinism, Pavlovian conditioning—all served to create an illusion of a social science indistinguishable from natural science. In the nineteenth century, as well as the early twentieth, most intellectuals aspired to scientific status. Scientific boosterism as personified by Huxley dominated intellectual inquiry. The advance of science required a recasting of man's nature. Notions of human reason and freedom were repugnant because they were the major basis for denying an easy equation of social with natural science. If man possessed freedom and reason, then social science had no place to stand. Or at least so it was, and sometimes still is, mistakenly thought. Enrico Ferri, in a remarkable show of candor rarely evident among his unwitting contemporary followers, appends the following argument to his pathetically inept demonstration that statistics prove the non-existence of free choice. One can hardly resist the observation that *this* and not the dubious statistical argument was the real foundation for the premature liquidation of human reason and freedom.

Furthermore, this moral liberty, if once admitted, would make all psychological and social science impossible and absurd in exactly the same way that the supposition of free choice in the atoms of matter would destroy all physical and chemical science. Hence, the negation of free choice instead of being, as the spiritual schools assert, the source of all evils, is fertile in its beneficent effects in moral and social life, since it teaches tolerance of ideas, inspires mutual indulgence and counsels. . . . Negation [of free will] is the necessary condition of all sociological theory and practice.[8]

Thus it was believed that social science required the negation of choice. What better group to start with than criminals? Surely they did not possess reason. And to deny them freedom was not without its compensations. Indeed, the needs of the new scientific disciplines coincided with the preachings of compassionate humanitarians. The negation of freedom not only suited the pretensions and ambitions of social science; it also was a fundamental requirement of a view that commended the treatment of criminals. Persons without choice are not responsible for their actions. Instead of punishment, they require treatment or other forms of correction. Thus, the joining of determinism as a heuristic principle motivating the analyst to profound inquiry with determinism as a model of human nature was expedited by the needs of emergent professions and humane liberalism. But what of man's nature, generally, and criminal nature, specifically? Did they too warrant the negation of the principle of human choice?

The view of modern social science is fairly complex and by no means unified or definitive. Whatever the ambiguities, however, a shift to a softer determinism is clearly discernible. The crucial step—a breaking of the link between directives for the analyst and the nature of the object of inquiry—has been taken. Indeed, soft determinism may be defined as the maintaining of the principle of universal causality as a guide to profound inquiry and an abandoning of universal assumptions regarding the nature of man, criminal or otherwise. Man's nature with respect to reason and freedom, it is nowadays conceded, is after all an empirical question that can be expected to yield characteristically variable answers. Men vacillate between choice and constraint.

Man is neither as free as he feels nor as bound as he fears. There are some aspects of himself, as of his environment, which he may easily transform, some aspects which he may transform only with difficulty and others which he can never transform. . . . Much of the debate concerning the freedom of the will arose from a confusion between the concepts of causality and freedom and from a derivative failure to distinguish motives that are more free from motives that are less free. . . . The conventional concept of causality, which generated the pseudo problem of the freedom of the will, assumed that the relationship between events was essentially two-valued, either determinate or capricious, and that man's will was therefore either slavishly determined or capriciously free. We feel, however, that this controversy concerns man's degree of freedom rather than the determinateness of his behavior.[9]

Moreover, some men are apparently freer than others. The degree of freedom possessed by different men is far from indeterminate. Freedom, like most social qualities is not randomly distributed. Though each is in some measure constrained, emperor and slave are not equally constrained. Each evades the limits of unfettered freedom and complete constraint, but that should not obscure the great differences between the two.

An agent . . . is constrained in so far as some power outside himself prevents him from doing what he wants to do. When a man wills something he acts on the assumption that his objective is attainable. If someone forbids him to pursue this objective or compels him to do something he does not want to do, then he is constrained, he is in this respect no longer free. But he still retains some freedom to act and to will. Even the slave has some freedom, has some alternatives between which to choose. Even if he decides to die rather than to live, or to suffer punishment rather than to obey, he is choosing between available alternatives and is to that extent free. His freedom is grossly limited but is not utterly abolished. The amount of freedom a man has is always a matter of degree. An emperor and slave have different degrees of freedom. The one can perform many voluntary acts, the other only a few. Freedom exists as long as restraint is not total.[10]

The essential elements of the position of soft determinism are even more succinctly put by an opposition spokesman.

According to [soft determinism] there is . . . no contradiction whatsoever between determinism and the proposition that human beings are sometimes free agents. When we call an action "free" we mean that the agent was not compelled or constrained to perform it. Sometimes people act in a certain way because of threats or because they have been drugged or because of a posthypnotic suggestion or because of an irrational overpowering urge that makes a kleptomaniac steal something he does not really need. On such occasions human beings are not free agents. But on other occasions they act in certain ways because of their own rational desires, because of their unimpeded efforts, because they have chosen to act in these ways. On those occasions they are free agents although their actions are just as much caused as actions that are deemed free. In distinguishing between free and unfree actions we do not try to mark the presence and absence of causes but attempt to indicate the *kind* of causes that are present.[11]

The fundamental assertion of soft determinism is that human actions are not deprived of freedom because they are causally determined. The compromise of soft determinism is not without difficulties. The hard determinist, not without sense, reasons as follows:

If the decision that characterizes voluntary actions is itself determined, so that given the whole situation it could not be otherwise, then the choice between alternatives is illusory. A man acts as he must act, chooses as he must choose, decides as he must decide.[12]

The answer of the soft determinists has two elements, one more celebrated than the other. The first element consisted of the long overdue recognition that man was after all different from the chemical and physical particles analyzed by natural scientists. Virtually no reputable social scientist today would flat-footedly propound a Law of Criminal Saturation in which Ferri proclaimed:

The level of crime each year is determined by the different conditions of the physical and social environment combined with the congenital tendencies and accidental impulses of individuals, in accordance with a law, which, in analogy to the law of chemistry, I have called the law of criminal saturation. As a given volume of water at a definite temperature will dissolve a fixed quantity of chemical substance and not an atom more or less; so in a given social environment with definite individual and physical conditions, a fixed number of delicts, no more and no less, can be committed.[13]

The distinctive quality of a science of man has been put in many ways but each stresses the necessity of adapting the science to the unique characteristics of the object of inquiry—man. Weber stressed the subjective element of human action and thus the mandatory element of *verstehen*.[14] MacIver distinguishes between different causal realms. Man may be found in the realm of the teleological nexus. Since man is purposive, causal analysis of his behavior may not ignore the goals he poses and the means he uses. "Those who oppose determinism to 'free will,'" suggests MacIver, "are apt to forget that human beings, as individuals and as groups are themselves dynamic participants within the causal order." [15] Man does not occupy a place in the sheerly physical realm of invariant order, adds MacIver. The language of stimulus-response is misleading. "Such language does not concede to the conscious agent any initiative or efficacy." [16]

The second element underlying the soft determinist position is often subdued. It consists of the recognition of the rather flimsy basis for the defense of determinism even as a directive for analysis. No longer certain of universal causality itself, the soft determinist is unwilling to allow a heuristic principle to shape his perception of man and to offend his common-sense perceptions. Determinism has been under attack in physical science. The social scientist has responded to the uncertainty regarding the principle of determinism primarily through limiting its consequences. He retains it merely as a motivation to seek deeper and deeper explanations of phenomena.

Currently, determinism is seen for what it is—a faith. In the physical sciences, it is a shaky but still defensible faith. Though some physical events may be indeterminate, many obviously are not. In the social sciences, determinism has never been based on anything but sheer faith eternally "dealing in the I.O.U.s and promissory notes of hypotheticals." [17] The current status of determinism and indeterminism has been briefly summarized by Sidney Hook.

Indeterminism entails unpredictability in respect to a character or event assumed to be undetermined. . . . Unpredictability, however, does not entail indeterminism, since it is compatible with the existence of a theoretically determined system of such vast complexity that it is beyond human power to make correct predictions. This raises a problem. What is the pragmatic difference between asserting that a system or state of affairs is undetermined and asserting that the system is so complexly determined that no predictions can be reliably made? If one must choose between these two assertions, it is reasonable to defend the assertion that the apparently undetermined system is actually a complexly determined one on *heuristic* grounds. If we act on the assumption that the system is determined, then it is more likely that we shall discover laws and make successful predictions . . . than if we assume that chance reigns. But can anything more than this be said for the belief in determinism? It does not carry us beyond Pierce's observation that determinism is a postulate, and a postulate is something we *hope* is true. . . . We can definitely reject indeterminism as false if it asserts that nothing is determined, because we know some things are; but if it asserts merely that not everything is determined, it cannot be rejected out of hand.[18]

The uncertainty regarding the postulate of universal causality has resulted in a more voluntaristic conception of man. Since man occupies a position in a complex and loosely organized social system, since he is the object of unclear and often conflicting forces, and since he is himself an integral part of his social system, he possesses some leeway of choice. He acts, and his actions are variably free. The hard determinism of early sociology has been abandoned generally but not everywhere. In criminology, insulated as it has been from modern intellectual currents, the older notions of hard determinism have continued to shape our conceptions of human action. The positive delinquent does not exercise choice. Instead, his action is constrained. He must behave in a delinquent manner because of the determinants that have shaped him. A neoclassic revision of the conception of man has taken place and positive criminology has been more or less oblivious to it.

The third and final assumption of positive criminology was implicit in the conception of the constrained delinquent. The delinquent was fundamentally different from the law-abiding. This conception too has persistently shaped the positivist image of delinquency. Differentiation is the favored method of positivist explanation. Each school of positive criminology has pursued its own theory of differentiation between conventional and criminal persons. Each in turn has regularly tended to exaggerate these differences. At its inception positive criminology revolted against the assumption of the general similarity between criminal and conventional persons implicit in classical theory. In rejecting the obviously untenable classical conception of similarity, positive criminology characteristically proceeded to the other extreme—radical differentiation—and in a variety of guises has persisted in this caricature. From the born criminal to differential association, the explanation of delinquency has rested in the radically different circumstances experienced by delinquent and law-abiding alike. Each is constrained, but by a fundamentally different set of circumstances.

Bentham and other classicists stressed the nature and effects of criminal law and procedure. Their picture of the criminal was not highly developed. He was at least by implication pretty much like other people. Modern criminologists consistently point to this characteristic of classical thought as being among its fundamental shortcomings.

The problem of why certain persons pursue criminal patterns in their quest for happiness while others do not is not considered deeply by Bentham. His only answer would seem to be that the external given situation is such that, without adequate deterrence (pain), any person in the situation would act in a criminal manner. This fails to take cognizance of the variations in the individuals facing the given situation. It is not the individuals who vary, Bentham believed, but the situations which are different.[19]

A reliance on differentiation, whether constitutional, personal, or sociocultural, as the key explanation of delinquency has pushed the standard-bearers of diverse theories to posit what have almost always turned out to be empirically undemonstrable differences.

Developments in Positive Criminology

There have been many occasions in which specific theories regarding the determinants of delinquency have been criticized, attacked, and shown inadequate. Indeed, the history of positive criminology is in large part an elaboration of specific sets of determinants, a questioning of the efficacy of those factors, an abandoning of them, a period of indecision, and then a substitution of a new theory based on another set of determinants. Throughout, however (except during the period of indecision), the conceptions of constraint and differentiation prevail and the belief persists that the invariant conditions productive of delinquency have been or can be stated. Thus, despite the many disagreements regarding the sources of delinquent action, some of which culminate in bitter and vindictive polemic, a stable picture of the delinquent has remained. The conflicting theories have varied in many ways: in the specific determinants propounded, the number of factors specified, the diversity of academic disciplines represented, and the claims to definitiveness made by the author. But these variations should not mislead us. All are positivistic in their basic conceptions regarding the character of criminological enterprise and the nature of the object of their inquiry. Multifactor theories are as committed to the picture of the positive delinquent as monistic theories; representative bio-psycho-socio-economic theories are as committed as arrogantly psychiatric theory; modest theorists who dutifully admit the relevance of other factors are as committed as those who brashly deny the necessity of other conditions. The reader must grasp this point before proceeding. All schools of modern criminology believe in the positive delinquent. "All contemporary scientific criminology is positivistic in method and in basic formulations." [20] Both its theory stressing the study of determinants and its practice stressing a treatment approach are based on the underlying conceptions inherent in a picture of the positive delinquent. There are many different theories but they share similar preconceptions. Because they have developed within the insulated province of professional criminology, the theories have remained oblivious to the partial restoration of classical man implicit in the tentative victory of soft over hard determinism.

The earliest theories of positive criminology bore a certain resemblance to the notions of demonology which stressed the relation between deviation and possession by supernatural forces. Between positive criminology and the belief in possession came the classical view that posited both choice and the reign of natural forces. "Classical theories . . . represent an abandoning of the supernatural as a principle of explanation and as a guide to criminal procedure." [21] Positive criminology maintained and extended the naturalism of Beccaria and Bentham. The idea of possession, however, returned in natural garb. Fatalism became determinism. Biological forces substituted for the earlier demons. Man was a

creature of heredity. His behavior, however laudable or repre-
hensible, was a playing out of genetic forces. The predominantly
biological origin of positive criminology must be noted because
of the continuing effect it has had on the nature of criminological
thought. In fact, we have no control over the consequences of
genetic circumstance. If biological theories had been victorious,
the assumption of criminal constraint would have been eminently
warranted. However, when the factors deemed operative shifted
radically from the biological to personal or social circumstance,
the assumption of constraint was allowed to lie implicit. Once
implicit and thus not subjected to discussion and revision, the
contemporary view that sociocultural or psychic determinants
control and constrain behavior in the same sense and the same
measure as genetic determinants could emerge. It emerged not
because anyone explicitly declared it or defended it but because
no one bothered to revise the conception of constraint when social
and psychic theories became ascendant.

Biological theories seek the origins of delinquency in the physiological constitution of the offender. Most often these theories
have stressed inherited characteristics, though some have empha-
sized the importance of postnatal trauma, injury, or disfigure-
ment.[22] A great variety of constitutional factors have been considered. Among them have been head size, endocrine balance,
character of the nervous system, body type, and intelligence. Attempts to designate a specific causal agent failed, and consequently a diffuse nomenclature became characteristic of biological
theories. Allegedly causal agents have included

a taint, a determinant natural predisposition, a psychopathic predisposition, a neuropathic constitution, a tendency to degeneration, a
feeble inhibition, a special recessive Mendelian character, a neuronal
factor, an anatomic trait, a neuropathic diathesis, a diminished germinal
vitality, a vitiation of the germ plasm, a cerebral infirmity, a germinal
enmity, and an unstable nervous organization.[23]

The logic of the biological argument is straightforward. It
views man, criminal or not, as an organic being, "born with more
or less immutable organic structure, functioning within the limits
of his genetic structure under the influence of his environment." [24]
Thus, there is a general relationship between morphology and

function—between man's constitution and his behavior. Since crime is merely a form of behavior, we may conclude that there is a constitutional basis for criminal behavior whatever other factors play a role.

The passing of biological theories of crime—from a period when they were dominant to contemporary times when, rightly or wrongly, a belief in them is used as an index of authoritarian personality—was part of the general decline of the biological explanation of human behavior.[25] The general decline of biological explanation was one of the key events in the study of man and society. This is surely not the place to describe that process. There were many reasons for the decline. Those that were intellectual rather than ideological were connected to the greater role allegedly played by the personal or sociocultural environment. Subsequently, new explanations replaced the generally discredited biological theories.

With the advent of environmental primacy, positive criminology has taken two major forms—one stressing intimate factors, the other, broader and wider events. Let us call the first personality theory and the second sociological. Compared to biological theories, a personality approach widens the circle of persons and events that are implicated in the onset of delinquency. But compared to sociological theories, the circle of implicated events and persons is fairly narrow. Though there is no clear dividing line between biological and personality theories just as there is none between personality and social theories, gross distinctions can be drawn and are perhaps helpful.

The defining characteristic of the biological approach is the view that the crucial predispositions to delinquency are *not* dependent on personal interaction. Instead, they are inherited or stem from various physiological defects, stigmata, or injuries. By contrast, the central thesis of personality theories is that a certain organization of personality developed in intimate interpersonal surroundings will result in criminal behavior.[26] Like their biological predecessors, few personality theorists deny the relevance of other factors. Thus, the argument is framed in probabilistic terms—delinquency is a necessary or almost necessary outgrowth of a particular personality pattern. But the probabilistic construction is *not* a compromise with the belief in the constrained delinquent. Rather, it is a reluctant bow to the minimal legitimacy of colleagues in other academic departments, and also another promissory note in the form of the humble confession that all is not yet known. The notion that the delinquent's behavior is really constrained is firmly implanted in the presumptions of theory and research and it is projected on to the object of inquiry, thus coloring for better or worse our picture of the real thing.

The logic of the argument in a personality theory of delinquency is clear and by no means implausible. Behavior at any given moment in time, whatever its character, is a function of key personal relationships and concomitant emotional states appearing during one's biography. To the extent that behavior is governed by personality, contemporary situations are important only in that they remind us of previous events and thus elicit appropriate responses. This does not rule out the relevance of other situational factors; it merely relegates them to a secondary position.

From the plethora of biographical events, *initial* sets of experiences play a key role in subsequent perception and behavior in that they provide persisting sets, predispositions and self-images that are used in the perception of and response to various situations confronted by the actor. The key role performed by the pattern of initial experience is that it indicates a line of action to the child, and, when reinforced as normally occurs, it compels a line of action. Initial sets of experiences consist wholly or mostly of intimate relations within the family, either between parents and child or among siblings. Thus, personality patterns are set within the familial milieu. Extrafamilial figures may play a role in the setting of personality pattern but only insofar as they too enter into intimate and symbolically infused relationships with the child. To the extent that the family does not enjoy a monopoly of initial intimacy, other figures may be implicated in the molding of a delinquent personality pattern.

Delinquency is a form of behavior. It is a pattern of response that is most frequently characterized by personality theorists as aggressive and antisocial. However, delinquent action is not merely a response to an immediate situation. Rather it is an acting out of a disorganized or malformed personality. The immediate situation serves only to touch off or elicit predispositions which are latent in the delinquent. As in biological theories, the specific factors determining delinquency are many and diffusely described. Delinquency results from an aggressive or antisocial personality arising out of parental neglect, or perhaps overindulgence, or perhaps inconsistency; from a delinquent self-image arising out of criminal or delinquent role models, or perhaps an overbearing maternal figure who for reasons of her own encourages or too vehemently discourages antisocial behavior; from specific neurotic syndromes—different delinquencies being manifestations of different neuroses; from the failure of parents to adequately socialize their children—delinquency being merely infantile, presocialized behavior; from an attenuation of the ego culminating in an inability to fathom the realistic consequences of transgression and an incapacity to resist the lure of companions.

The distinguishing feature of sociological theory, in contrast to formulations stressing personality, lies in the prominence of the social situation. Sociology brings to the foreground the social circumstances that form the backdrop for personality theory. The initial and persistent basis for a social theory of delinquency, both in its formulations and its critiques of other theories, is epidemiology—the study of contrasting rates of pathology in different social areas. Social theory begins with the observation that there are gross differences in the rate of delinquency by class, by ethnic affiliation, by rural or urban residence, by region, and perhaps by nation and historical epoch. From these gross differences, the sociologist infers that something beyond the intimacy of family surroundings is operative in the emergence of delinquent patterns; something in the cultural and social atmosphere apparent in certain sectors of society.

Thus, the basic effect of sociological theory has been to greatly widen the scope of persons and events that are implicated in the appearance of delinquency. Such events as far removed from the intimacy of the interpersonal milieu as immigration, economic cycle, war and peace, class background, and shifting cultural norms have been considered as possible sources of delinquent behavior. The sociological approach culminates in the vision of a relation between society and its delinquents. Delinquency, sociologically viewed, is a product of subtle and complex forces which are on the face of it far removed from the intimate surroundings or personal troubles of individual children. Indeed, the abnormal nature of the individual delinquent's constitution or personality is profoundly challenged. Individual abnormality remains a possibility, from the sociological perspective, but it is no more than that. What is axiomatic in the biological or personality view—individual pathology—is problematic for the sociologist. However, the attack on the concept of individual pathology should not mislead us into believing that sociologists do not picture the delinquent as being fundamentally different from conventional youth. The sociological study of delinquency has been no less affected by the presumptions of positive criminology than its biological and psychological competitors. Sociologists, too, driven by the distinctive method of positivism, have sought basic differences between delinquent and conventional children. Like the other disciplines sociology has exaggerated these differences in the interests of cogent and convincing theoretical explanation. The alleged differentiation claimed by diverse theorists representing each of the disciplines has rarely if ever been confirmed in empirical research.

For the sociologist, the nature of constraint is not compulsion as in biological or personality theory, and the basis of differentiation is not individual pathology. Rather the delinquent as portrayed in sociological theory is constrained through commitment to an ethical code which makes his misdeeds mandatory.[27] The delinquent, according to contemporary sociological theory, is a rather normal youngster—except that he belongs to what is essentially a different though related culture. Instead of learning our precepts, he learns others. It is ironic that the sociological view which began as a protest against the conviction that the delinquent was something apart has managed again to thrust the delinquent outside the pale of normal social life. Such is the force of the positivist determination to find and accentuate differences.

The logic of the sociological argument is, like those already described, plausible. The argument begins by asserting that values and norms serve as directives to action and that, despite the complexity involved in the emergence of beliefs, once present they commit adherents to lines of action; this, irrespective of whether the adherents have in one manner or another recapitulated the collective experiences productive of those beliefs. Thus, in the language of positivism, beliefs are an independent variable. In the most influential expressions of contemporary sociological theory of delinquency, *beliefs*, delinquent ones, are the key independent variable.[28] Delinquency is fundamentally the translation of beliefs to action. There are many variants of this formulation and there are many disputes. But the disputes center on the process by which delinquents come to have such peculiar commitments.

Because of the key role played by beliefs in the determination of delinquency and because delinquent beliefs are so radically different from those of conventional youth, it more or less follows that *subculture* is a most propitious level at which to begin analysis. It is quite fair to say that subculture is *the* central idea of the dominant sociological view of delinquency. To proceed to lower levels or smaller groupings, except as intervening agencies or transmission belts, has seemed largely unnecessary in that the increments of predictability hardly seem to warrant the additional effort expended. The carrier of the delinquent code is a group of peers or perhaps a neighborhood, but little is added to the basic theory by the description of such entities since their function is merely to transmit to the individual neophyte a set of beliefs that are traditionally implanted in a certain section of society—by general consensus, the slum. Peers are for the sociologist what families are for the personality theorist. They represent the intimate setting within which delinquent impulses are transmitted and generated.

Just as levels below that of subculture play no significant role in the contemporary sociological theory of delinquency, so too more abstruse levels like the wider culture are irrelevant except as a kind of diffuse backdrop against which the delinquent figure may be spotlighted and from which the delinquent subculture has allegedly become differentiated. Here is the dominant culture of modern America—ranging in its portrayal from ascetic puritanism to the oath of boy scouts—and here is the subculture of delinquency, so antithetical to conventional belief that, given its precepts, delinquency is mandatory. Whatever else the reader may infer from the contemporary sociological portrayal, he is sure

to be convinced of the fundamental difference between the delinquent's subculture and the wider culture of conventional American youth.

The adherents of the delinquent subculture, characteristically
slum youth, learn the precepts of their society in a manner not
markedly different from that involved in the learning of conventional ways. According to some theorists, they must first locate
each other through a variety of cues, but others, perhaps the
majority, believe that in the slum adherents are in such great
supply that the burden of location falls on the few who somehow
accommodate by anticipation to the standards of middle-class
morality. Thus, delinquents learn in a crimogenic milieu just as
we learn in one that is conventionally oriented. In the language
of Sutherland, it is a matter of "differential association." [29] The
propensity to associate may arise from sheer propinquity in the
case of children who grow up in tough delinquent areas, or it may
follow a period of alienation from family, school, and other agents
of law and order.

The forces that produce delinquent beliefs vary depending on
the sociological observer. Some posit one or another frustration
or resentment as the source of delinquent beliefs; inflexible scholastic standards which favor middle-class youth; the inability of
working class youth to effectively compete for status with better-
trained boys in more privileged sectors of society; the belief of
working-class schoolboys that opportunities do not await them
upon graduation; the prolonged period of abstinence allegedly
required during adolescence; the discriminatory treatment of new
ethnics, or the conflicts and marginality experienced by the second
generation of immigrants. Other theories focus on the delinquent
consequences of disorganization in certain neighborhoods; the
breakdown of community and family organization; the corruption
of legal authority by syndicates organized around the dispensing
of vice; the emergence of a crimogenic milieu within which juvenile delinquency flourishes. Finally, the view of cultural anthropology alleges that members of the working classes happen
to have different autonomous traditions. Unfortunately, these
exist in a society rather given to others—the traditions implicit
in middle-class morality. This, as we might expect, leads to trouble.

Despite the diversity of opinions regarding the source, the most influential of contemporary sociological theorists arrive at a remarkably similar picture of the delinquent. He is committed to delinquency through membership in a subculture that requires the breaking of laws. The sociological delinquent is trapped by the accident of membership, just as his predecessors were trapped by the accident of hereditary defect or emotional disturbance. The delinquent has come a long way under the auspices of positive criminology. He has been transformed from a defective to a defector.

Positivism assumes that delinquency, like any other human or physical action, is constrained. How can we know whether this assumption is warranted or not? There is no certain way because hard determinism is a faith whose peculiar utopia is prediction and control. A faith is not capable of empirical test, but it may be tentatively assessed according to its consequences. My suggestion is that the consequence of hard determinism has been to push criminologists toward a distorted and misleading picture of the delinquent and his enterprise.

The conventional criticisms of each theory of delinquency—and each has its critics—have dealt with the problem of insufficiency or inadequacy. Each theory, argues its critic—and always correctly —falls short of the standards of science in that delinquency remains inadequately explained. Since the conditions of necessity of sufficiency are not met, delinquency cannot be predicted from the factors specified by the theory. This line of attack is a positivist criticism of a similarly inclined theory and is certainly appropriate and warranted. However, other lines of attack are possible. If one assumes, as I wish to, that delinquents are not wholly constrained and not markedly different, then the conventional criticisms may be augmented. By assuming constraint and differentiation—by ignoring choice and similarity—positive criminology leaves unexplained commonplace and consistent features of delinquent life.

An Embarrassment of Riches

Positive criminology accounts for too much delinquency. Taken at their terms, delinquency theories seem to predicate far more delinquency than actually occurs. If delinquents were in fact radically differentiated from the rest of conventional youth in that their unseemly behavior was constrained through compulsion or commitment, then involvement in delinquency would be more permanent and less transient, more pervasive and less intermittent than is apparently the case. Theories of delinquency yield an embarrassment of riches which seemingly go unmatched in the real world. This accounting for too much delinquency may be taken as an observable consequence of the distorted picture of the delinquent that has developed within positive criminology.

Given the assumptions of constraint and differentiation, the frequency with which delinquents more or less reform is most perplexing. "Most juvenile delinquents outgrow their delinquencies. Relatively few become adult offenders. They grow up, come to terms with their world, find a job or enter the armed forces, get married and indulge in . . . only an occasional spree." [30] Anywhere from 60 to 85 per cent of delinquents do not apparently become adult violators. Moreover, this reform seems to occur irrespective of intervention of correctional agencies and irrespective of the quality of correctional service.[31]

Most theories of delinquency take no account of maturational reform; those that do often do so at the expense of violating their own assumptions regarding the constrained delinquent. Why and by what process do youngsters once compelled or committed to delinquency cease being constrained? Why and by what process is the easy continuity from juvenile delinquency to adult crime implicit in almost all theories of delinquency not apparent in the world of real events? [32] Biological theories are hardest hit by the frequency of maturational reform if only because the compulsion of biological constraint has a more literal meaning than psychic or social constraint and has been so taken. What is it that happens to body type, endocrine balance, or neuropathic diathesis at approximately age 20 that is related to reform? Once such questions are posed, the proponents of each theory are quick to qualify and add as afterthoughts clauses whose function is to salvage the positivist conception of constraint. They may point, for instance, to the especially turbulent consequences of pubescence. Unfortunately, the number of additional clauses mounts with each happening that is brought to attention, and the end result comes to resemble the pre-Copernican epicyclic path traversed by the sun around the earth—a path that was at best inelegant and at worst misleading. This tendency to salvage preconceptions by adding to the multitude of relevant factors is characteristic of positive criminology.

Whenever objections are raised about a specific viewpoint or more fundamental objections about the preconceptions of positive criminology, serious discussion and scrutiny is evaded by the seemingly frank and humble admission that "other factors are operative." The principle of multicausation may be an honorable heuristic device. But it may also become a powerful force for intellectual inertia. It may point the way to new discoveries. Or it may allow discussants to dodge the necessity of a serious reappraisal of the nature of their object of study. Whether the principle of multicausation is a legitimate heuristic device or a way of avoiding the implications of negative evidence depends, partially, on the number of factors invoked.

A theory is not judged only by its predictiveness. Even if delinquency could be predicted, and, given the current state of knowledge, it obviously cannot, still we would desire more. Theory should be elegant and parsimonious and not simply for reasons of esthetic sensibility. When theories are cumbersome, this may be a sign of a rather fundamental misconception. When many factors matter rather than few, and no one can pretend to know how many is too many, this may be a signal that our model is not a truthful simplifying of reality but instead a complicated falsification. A cumbersome multifactor theory is not necessarily a sign of misconception. A science of man may differ fundamentally from natural science in the simplicity with which it may be rendered. But, so too, may it differ in the extent to which its object of inquiry, man, is constrained. Given the current state of knowledge, we are free to choose.

A principle of multicausation has other defects. When factors become too numerous, there is a tendency for them to be not factors at all, but rather contingencies. The term factor after all means something. A factor is a condition that is applicable to a given universe. It has an effect on everyone, not equally to be sure but according to degree. It is not something that may or may not matter. Factors may matter to varying extents, but every factor must by definition matter to some extent. Is the way in which a policeman responded to a child on their first meeting a factor? Does it matter or not? Is American foreign policy a factor? Does it matter or not? Is the demeanor of a child's sixth-grade teacher a factor? Does it matter or not? And so on, endlessly. Common sense tells us that these occurrences may matter, or not, depending on many other things that may more legitimately be considered factors. Some occurrences may or may not matter. Thus, they are contingencies and not factors. If we insist on considering them factors, we are in the hopeless position of arguing that everything matters. The tendency to continually add to the multitude of relevant factors has been characteristic of positive criminology.

Personality theories, save those specifically based on the disturbances of adolescence, fare only slightly better than biological theories in avoiding the embarrassment of improper accounting. The reformed delinquent, untouched as he normally is by therapeutic hands, simply eludes explanation in terms of personality theory. Surely, the emotional disorders stressed by personality theorists and the ensuing patterns of aggressive or asocial personality do not simply vanish or even subside with the coming of adulthood. Personality theory offers no explanation, but proponents of this view, particularly practitioners, are cognizant of the frequency of maturational reform. Consequently, a number of concepts have arisen which leave the impression of explanation. Actually, they are only a recognition of the problem. A notion like "burning out" merely reiterates the occurrence of maturational reform. It hardly explains it. The notion of "adolescent maladjustment" which purports to be a diagnostic category is for the most part a simple reiteration of the juvenile's delinquency. Adolescent maladjustment has replaced the term "psychopath" in the juvenile correctional institution. It is a summary way of stating that there seems to be little difference between this lad and most conventional youth, but there obviously is some difference since here he is in serious trouble. A variable but high proportion of juveniles who appear before the court or are in institutions are "diagnosed" as having adolescent maladjustment.

Sociological theories, save those focusing on the tribulations of adolescence, do no better in accounting for maturational reform. Perhaps the most prominent contemporary sociological theory of delinquency—the theory of subcultural delinquency, of which there are many variants—finds it especially difficult to explain maturational reform. This subculture, as is elaborated in the following chapter, consists of juveniles who are allegedly committed to a set of beliefs that propels them to delinquent deeds. If this allegation is warranted, why and by what process are these beliefs set aside at the age of remission? Are norms and sentiments once deeply cherished so easily set aside? Beliefs are sometimes shed and new ones taken in their place, but ordinarily such shifts imply rather fundamental moral conversion. Nowhere in the accounts of the delinquent subculture do we read of crisis, reevaluation of commitment, and other normal concomitants of moral conversion. Thus, there is reason to doubt the dedication with which the subcultural delinquent pursues and perpetrates his misdeeds. Once dedication or commitment is rendered dubious, the contemporary sociological theory of delinquency loses much of its initial plausibility, for it is commitment that is the motive force in activating the behavior presumably explained.

Whatever the character of the underlying determinants, contemporary sociological theory posits a set of intervening *beliefs* which shape the perception and ultimately the behavior of delinquents. The conditions that produce delinquent beliefs differ according to the specific writer, but whatever their character, the conditions make their direct impact on groups through the peculiar norms, sentiments, and outlooks they produce. Thus, contemporary sociological theory of delinquency is almost always sociocultural in character. It specifies the structural dislocations that engender peculiar subcultural adaptations. The ideas and practices that are transmitted within groups and neighborhoods occupy a strategic position in the sociological view of delinquency. Because the notion of commitment albeit to deviant ideas and practices is central to the sociological view, it faces theoretical problems that are roughly similar to those of biological or personality theory of delinquency. The major difference is that commitment rather than compulsion is the constraining force—the determinant. The problem is that the constraint seems regularly and persistently to vanish with the coming of adulthood. The determinants along with the theories that espouse them apparently suffer a diminishing of potency with the sheer passage of time.

Just as the frequency of maturational reform may indicate that current theories of delinquency predict far too much delinquency over lifetimes, so too the frequency of the delinquent's conformity to both conventional and unconventional standards may suggest that these same theories predict too much delinquency even during the period of optimum involvement. Delinquency is after all a legal status and not a person perpetually breaking laws. A delinquent is a youngster who in relative terms more warrants that legal appellation than one who is less delinquent or not at all so. He is a delinquent by and large because the shoe fits, but even so we must never imagine that he wears it very much of the time. Delinquency is a status and delinquents are incumbents who *intermittently* act out a role. When we focus on the incumbents rather than the status, we find that most are perfectly capable of conventional activity. Thus, delinquents intermittently play both delinquent and conventional roles. They play or act well in both situations. The novice practitioner or researcher is frequently amazed at "how like other kids" the delinquent can be when he is so inclined.

Moreover, the delinquent conforms to the unconventional standards of peer groups.[33] Sustained patterns of disapproved conduct, and surely delinquency is one, flourish best within a context of peers—persons of generally similar circumstance, propensity, and destiny.

The conformity of delinquents to the unconventional standards of their peers—their minimal capacity to behave civilly—is no embarrassment to sociological theories of delinquency. On the contrary, it is their point of departure. For biological and personality theories, however, it should be a source of considerable embarrassment since it means that whatever inner drive compels the delinquent is capable of recurrent and systematic internal control. Rebelliousness, aggressiveness, impulsiveness, or whatever, are barely evident within appropriate contexts like gang-meetings or visits with conventional adults. Thieves no doubt fall out—one need not romanticize the order and loyalty of delinquent groups to suggest their considerable capacity in overcoming alleged delinquent constraints.

A standard criticism of biological and personality theories made by sociologists pertains to the delinquent's ability to conform albeit to unconventional expectations. This point is essential to the sociological argument and is a telling one. But by the same token, how account for the delinquent's frequent conformity to the standards and expectations he allegedly repudiates? [34] If his conventional behavior were merely tactical—something to be done in the presence of authorities—there would be little problem, but this hardly seems an adequate accounting. The delinquent joins settlement houses—when he is permitted to—he plays on ball teams, belongs to youth organizations like the boy scouts, and even welcomes detached emissaries (i.e., gang workers) from the conventional world whose avowed and publicized purpose is his conversion. He is, in other words, quite amenable to agents of the conventional order. Not only can the delinquent negate the forces that presumably constrain him to offend for tactical reasons—which in itself is quite telling—he also commonly indulges in mundane and commonplace childhood activity. He is very much capable of civil behavior and our understandable focus on his deviance has obscured this otherwise obvious point. The alleged delinquent constraints are in the normal course of his life somehow rendered inoperative. Current theories of delinquency, because they have maintained the positivist assumptions of constraint and differentiation, may explain although always inadequately the juvenile's deviance, but at the cost of leaving us bewildered by his commonplace behavior.

Delinquent Drift: An Alternative Image

An alternative image of the delinquent can be developed by accepting the implications of soft rather than hard determinism. One effect of restoring choice to man is to render feasible a joining of classical with positivist assumptions. I wish to maintain the spirit of positive inquiry but to suggest certain modifications of its picture of the delinquent. These modifications consistently follow lines implicit in the classic criminological view.

Some men are freer than others. Most men, including delinquents, are neither wholly free nor completely constrained but fall somewhere between. The general conditions underlying various positions along a continuum from freedom to constraint may be described. Viewed in this way, determinism loses none of its heuristic value. We may still act as if all were knowable, but we refrain at least temporarily from an image of the delinquent that is tailored to suit social science. The image of the delinquent I wish to convey is one of drift; an actor neither compelled nor committed to deeds nor freely choosing them; neither different in any simple or fundamental sense from the law abiding, nor the same; conforming to certain traditions in American life while partially unreceptive to other more conventional traditions; and finally, an actor whose motivational system may be explored along lines explicitly commended by classical criminology—his peculiar relation to legal institutions.

The delinquent is casually, intermittently, and transiently immersed in a pattern of illegal action. His investment of affect in the delinquent enterprise is sufficient so as to allow an eliciting of prestige and satisfaction but not so large as to "become more or less unavailable for other lines of action." [35] In point of fact, the delinquent is available even during the period of optimum involvement for many lines of legal and conventional action. Not only is he available but a moment's reflection tells us that, concomitant with his illegal involvement, he actively participates in a wide variety of conventional activity. If commitment implies, as it does, rendering oneself presently and in the future unavailable for other lines of action, then the delinquent is uncommitted. He is committed to neither delinquent nor conventional enterprise. Neither, by the canons of his ideology or the makeup of his personality, is precluded.

Drift stands midway between freedom and control. Its basis is an area of the social structure in which control has been loosened, coupled with the abortiveness of adolescent endeavor to organize an autonomous subculture, and thus an independent source of control, around illegal action. The delinquent *transiently* exists in a limbo between convention and crime, responding in turn to the demands of each, flirting now with one, now the other, but postponing commitment, evading decision. Thus, he drifts between criminal and conventional action.

To be loosened from control, conventional or delinquent, is not equivalent to freedom, and, thus, I do not propose a free or calculating actor as an alternative to constraint. Freedom is not only the loosening of controls. It is a sense of command over one's destiny, a capacity to formulate programs or projects, a feeling of being an agent in one's own behalf. Freedom is self-control. If so, the delinquent has clearly not achieved that state. The sense of self-control, irrespective of whether it is well founded, exists to varying degrees in modern man. Those who have been granted the potentiality for freedom through the loosening of social controls but who lack the position, capacity, or inclination to become agents in their own behalf, I call drifters, and it is in this category that I place the juvenile delinquent.

Drift is motion guided gently by underlying influences. The guidance is gentle and not constraining. The drift may be initiated or deflected by events so numerous as to defy codification. But underlying influences are operative nonetheless in that they make initiation to delinquency more probable, and they reduce the chances that an event will deflect the drifter from his delinquent path. Drift is a gradual process of movement, unperceived by the actor, in which the first stage may be accidental or unpredictable from the point of view of any theoretic frame of reference, and deflection from the delinquent path may be similarly accidental or unpredictable. This does not preclude a general theory of delinquency. However, the major purpose of such a theory is a description of the conditions that make delinquent drift possible and probable, and not a specification of invariant conditions of delinquency.

In developing an alternative picture, it should be obvious that not all delinquents correspond to the drifter here depicted. By hypothesis, most delinquents, although perhaps not most criminals, approximate the model. The delinquent as drifter more approximates the substantial majority of juvenile delinquents who do not become adult criminals than the minority who do. Some delinquents are neurotically compulsive and some in the course of their enterprise develop commitment. These flank the more ordinary delinquent on either side, and during situations of crisis perhaps play crucial leadership roles. Partially because he is more sensational and dramatic, the extraordinary delinquent has received greater attention in both mass media and criminological theory. The mundane delinquent is the exemplary delinquent in that he personifies, more fully than the compulsive or the committed, the spirit of the enterprise. The delinquent drifter is less likely to command our attention and we have partially ignored him. However, the drifter is not less a problem than the compulsive or committed delinquent even though he is far less likely to become an adult criminal. Though his tenure is short, his replacements are legion. Though his ideology does not make violations of personal and property rights mandatory, under certain conditions it condones them. Thus, what follows is not a plea for the delinquent but a plea for a reassessment of his enterprise.

NOTES

1. Histories of criminological theory may be found in Bernaldo de Quiros, *Modern Theories of Criminality,* Boston: Little Brown, 1911; George B. Vold, *Theoretical Criminology,* New York: Oxford University Press, 1958; Hermann Mannheim (editor), *Pioneers of Criminology,* Chicago: Quadrangle, 1960.
2. Clarence Ray Jeffrey, "The Historical Development of Criminology," in Mannheim, *op. cit.,* p. 377.
3. Vold, *op. cit.,* pp. 14–15.
4. Jeffrey, *op. cit.,* p. 379.
5. Vold, *op. cit.,* p. 14.
6. *Ibid.,* p. 26.
7. Cited in Paul Edwards, "Hard and Soft Determinism," in Sidney Hook (editor), *Determinism and Freedom in the Age of Modern Science,* New York: Collier, 1961, p. 120.
8. Enrico Ferri, *Criminal Sociology,* Boston: Little, Brown, 1917, pp. 297–298.
9. Silvan S. Tomkins, *Affect, Imagery, Consciousness: The Positive Affects,* Vol. 1, New York: Springer, 1962, pp. 108–109.
10. R. M. MacIver, *Social Causation,* Boston: Ginn, 1942, pp. 234–236.
11. Edwards, *op. cit.,* pp. 118–119.
12. MacIver, *loc. cit.*
13. Ferri, *op. cit.,* p. 209.
14. Max Weber, *The Methodology of Social Science,* Glencoe, Ill.: Free Press, 1949. The subjective or voluntaristic theory of action has been further developed in Kingsley Davis, *Human Society,* New York: Macmillan, 1948, Chap. 5, and in Talcott Parsons, *The Structure of Social Action,* New York: McGraw-Hill, 1937.
15. MacIver, *op. cit.* p. 236.
16. *Ibid.*
17. William Barrett, "Determinism and Novelty," in Hook, *op. cit.,* p. 48.
18. Sidney Hook, "Necessity, Indeterminism and Sentimentalism," in Hook, *op. cit.,* p. 180.
19. Gilbert Geis, "Jeremy Bentham," in Mannheim, *op. cit.,* p. 57.

20. Vold, *op. cit.*, p. 39.

21. *Ibid.*, p. 26.

22. Predominantly biological theories of crime include: Cesare Lombroso, *Criminal Man*, New York: Putnam, 1911; E. A. Hooton, *The American Criminal: An Anthropological Study*, Cambridge, Mass.: Harvard University Press, 1939. W. H. Sheldon, *Varieties of Delinquent Youth: An Introduction to Constitutional Psychiatry*, New York: Harper, 1949.

    Varying assessments of the biological view may be found in: William Tucker, "Is There Evidence for a Physical Basis of Criminal Behavior?," *Journal of Criminal Law and Criminology*, November–December 1940, pp. 427–437; Arthur Foxe, "Heredity and Crime," *Journal of Criminal Law and Criminology*, May–June 1945, pp. 11–16; W. Norwood East, "Physical Factors and Criminal Behavior," *Journal of Criminal Psychopathology*, October 1944, pp. 7–35; William McCord, "The Biological Basis of Juvenile Delinquency," in Joseph Roucek (editor), *Juvenile Delinquency*, New York: Philosophical Library, 1958.

23. Foxe, *loc. cit.*

24. Tucker, *loc. cit.*

25. Landmarks in the descent of biological theories of crime include: Gabriel Tarde, *Penal Philosophy*, Boston: Little, Brown, 1912; M. F. Ashley-Montagu, "The Biologist Looks at Crime," *Annals of the Academy of Political and Social Science*, September 1941, p. 217; Robert Merton and M. F. Ashley-Montagu, "Crime and the Anthropologist," *American Anthropologist*, August 1940, pp. 384–408.

26. Predominantly personality theories of crime may be found in: August Aichorn, *Wayward Youth*, New York: Viking, 1925; Robert Lindner, *Rebel Without a Cause*, New York: Grune and Stratton, 1944; Kate Friedlander, *The Psychoanalytic Approach to Juvenile Delinquency*, New York: International Universities Press, 1947; Kurt E. Eissler (editor), *Searchlights on Delinquency*, New York: International Universities Press, 1949; William Healy and Augusta Bronner, *New Light on Delinquency*, New Haven, Conn.: Yale University Press, 1936; Fritz Redl and David Wineman, *Children Who Hate*, Glencoe, Ill.: Free Press, 1951.

    Varying assessments of the personality view appear in: Karl Schuessler and Donald Cressey, "Personality Characteristics of Criminals" *American Journal of Sociology*, March 1950, pp. 476–484; Lucien Bovet, *Psychiatric Aspects of Juvenile Delinquency*, Geneva: World Health Organization, 1951; John W. McDavid and Boyd R. McCandless, "Psychological Theory, Research and Juvenile Delinquency," *Journal of Criminal Law, Criminology and Police Science*, March 1962, pp. 1–14.

27. The line of development stressing the insulated and autonomous quality of delinquent and criminal worlds proceeds from the Chicago ethnographic tradition exemplified in: Clifford Shaw, *The Natural History of a Delinquent Career*, Chicago: University of Chicago Press, 1931; Clifford Shaw, Henry McKay, and James McDonall, *Brothers in Crime*, Chicago: University of Chicago Press, 1938; Frederic M. Thrasher, *The Gang*, Chicago: University of Chicago Press, 1927.

It received additional momentum from the description of criminal tribes in Paul Cressey's "The Criminal Tribes of India," *Sociology and Social Research*, July–September 1936.

The view was further enhanced by works dealing with professional crime like Edwin H. Sutherland, *The Professional Thief*, Chicago: University of Chicago Press, 1937; and culminates in the contemporary view of subcultural delinquency as expressed by Albert Cohen, Lloyd Ohlin, Richard Cloward, Walter Miller, and others.

28. This view will be discussed in Chapter 2.
29. The most complete statement of this view may be found in Albert K. Cohen, Alfred Lindesmith, and Karl Schuessler (editors), *The Sutherland Papers*, Bloomington: Indiana University Press, 1956.
30. Jessie Bernard, *Social Problems at Midcentury*, New York: Dryden, 1957, pp. 421 and 444; William McCord, Joan McCord, and Irving Zola, *Origins of Crime*, New York: Columbia University Press, 1959, p. 21; W. H. Dunham and M. E. Knauer, "The Juvenile Court and Its Relationship to Adult Criminality," *Social Forces*, March 1954, pp. 290–296.
31. Edwin Powers and Helen Witmer, *An Experiment in the Prevention of Delinquency: The Cambridge-Somerville Youth Study*, New York: Columbia University Press, 1951; Dunham and Knauer, *loc. cit.;* Joan McCord and William McCord, "A Follow-up Report on the Cambridge-Somerville Youth Study," *The Annals of the American Academy of Political and Social Science*, March 1959, pp. 89–96.
32. A number of theories focusing specifically on adolescent problems are obviously not hurt by the frequency of maturational reform. For instance, Erik Erikson's thesis of identity crisis as developed in *New Perspectives for Research in Juvenile Delinquency*, edited by Helen Witmer and Ruth Kotinsky, Washington, D. C.: U. S. Department of Health, Education and Welfare, Children's Bureau Publication No. 356, 1956; also, Herbert Bloch and Arthur Niederhoffer, *The Gang*, New York: Philosophical Library, 1958.
33. The substance of these unconventional standards is the major topic of this book and will be discussed in later chapters. Suffice it to say now that these unconventional standards are not delinquent in the simple sense of that term.
34. Most modern writers and especially Albert Cohen have recognized the ambivalence that characterizes the delinquent. However, the implications of this ambivalence for our conceptions and theory of delinquency are not developed.
35. William Kornhauser, "Social Bases of Commitment: A Study of Liberals and Radicals," in Arnold M. Rose (editor), *Human Behavior and Social Processes*, Boston: Houghton Mifflin, 1962, pp. 321–322.

2

The Subculture of Delinquency

THERE is a subculture of delinquency, but it is not a delinquent subculture. That is the thesis of this chapter. The basic thesis of other writers is that of a delinquent subculture. Thus, the point at issue is the substance, or content, of the subculture of delinquency.

A subculture of delinquency is a setting in which the commission of delinquency is common knowledge among a group of juveniles. The size of the group varies—as a rule of thumb, let us say twice the number engaged in those delinquent acts requiring collective effort. The exact number is unimportant. What is important is publicity. Delinquency committed by lone offenders or by partners and cliques who hold a monopoly of knowledge regarding their delinquency is not subcultural. Subcultural delinquency is delinquency that is public within the confines of more or less provincial groupings. The defining characteristic is publicity; everything else is in the nature of hypothesis and thus open to dispute.

The delinquent subculture is the modern sociological rendition of the positivist assumptions regarding delinquency and crime. Juveniles may for a variety of reasons become adherents of the delinquent subculture, but once connected their delinquencies are explained as expressions of the peculiar standards which reign in that part of the world. Their behavior is determined by subculture as ours is by conventional culture. The precepts of the delinquent subculture are the immediate cause, according to current sociological theorists, of delinquent acts. All that intervenes between subcultural precept and delinquent act are the standard mechanisms of learning, conformity to reference group, and the seeking of status and reputation within that reference

33

group. It is in the peculiar subculture to which they owe allegiance that we may find the fundamental difference between juvenile delinquents and other youth. Their subcultural affiliations set them apart.

The major proponents of this theory vary in the clarity and the decisiveness with which they express the idea of a delinquent subculture. Albert Cohen hesitates, but finally portrays a delinquent subculture that is a reaction formation, an oppositional response to the pious legality of bourgeois existence. Though Cohen stresses the delinquent's ambivalence regarding middle-class morality, the ambivalence is resolved by the most radical of defense mechanisms—reaction formation. "Reaction-formation is stressed because it is not only a way of coming to terms with one's delinquent impulses; it helps to account for the nature of the delinquent behavior itself." [1] It may, but whether it does or not is precisely what is at issue. Reaction formation leading to an oppositional subculture may inform us of the "nature of the delinquent behavior itself," but it may also mislead us.

The delinquent's defense against the moral encroachments of the middle class is repudiation and a substitution of an inverted moral code celebrating malicious and hostile hedonism. Thus, the subcultural delinquent, according to Cohen, may begin with indecision or ambivalence, but he resolves it through commitment to moral negativism which is expressed in delinquent escapades. Delinquent action is the predictable outcome of the values, norms, and sentiments implicit in the delinquent subculture, as portrayed by Cohen. Cohen's image is one in which the delinquent considers his misdeeds praiseworthy if not good.[2]

Cohen is ambiguous on two critical points: the relation between delinquent and conventional values and the proximity between the values of delinquents and their behavior. This ambiguity, far from being a reason for criticism, is to Cohen's credit. His hesitancy reflects a sensibility to complexity which is less apparent in subsequent formulations. Subsequent developments of the theory of delinquent subculture posit an even more decisive break between delinquent and conventional values and a unity between the delinquent's theory and practice that would turn Marxists green with envy. Despite his guarded interpretation, however, Cohen finally implies that the relation between delinquent and conventional values is *oppositional,* and the relation between delinquent values and behavior is close. One cannot imagine how the values he attributes to the delinquent subculture could be adhered to without persistent and serious violation of law. Note that the two points on which Cohen hesitates and finally decides are precisely the distinguishing features of the sociological version of positive criminology—the radical distinction between the delinquent and conventional actors, and the determination of delinquency by normative constraint. I believe that Cohen is wrong on both these points and will suggest why in the following pages.

Albert Cohen's provocative *Delinquent Boys* elicited a great many responses; among these was a portrait of the delinquent subculture by Walter Miller.[3] Miller takes the postulates of differentiation and determinism implicit in the positivist approach to their sociological extreme. He suggests that lower class youth are virtually unaffected by the wider conventions of American society. They are members of an autonomous subculture with traditions of integrity and vintage.

Lower-class boys, argues Miller, are socialized in a habitat with standards and expectations that insist on behavior which is unfortunately unlawful from the point of view of conventional Americans. Lower-class boys are mindless of the legal code which is an expression of the morality of middle-class America except in that they cope with and resist the policemen who patrol their territory. They are as determined by their customs as we by ours. Miller's detailed and perceptive ethnography of slum life is consistently distorted by the interpretive framework in which it is set—a radical cultural determinism augmented by the ecologist's belief that the territorial boundaries of state and nation are political fictions of little social consequence.

Thus, Miller suggests that delinquent behavior can be directly inferred from what he calls "lower class culture." It is customary action that is delinquent only because the legal system reflects another more dominant value system. He says, "Following cultural practices which comprise essential elements of the total life pattern of lower class culture *automatically* [italics added] violates certain legal norms." [4] It is clear from the rest of Miller's argument that he does not refer to trivial violations, but to the full gamut of violations ordinarily associated with delinquency. For

Miller, delinquency and lower-class culture are one and the same thing. In a moment of caution, Miller almost retreats, but in the middle of the sentence seems to decide against it. He suggests, "In instances where alternative avenues to similar objectives are available, the non-law-abiding avenue frequently provides a relatively greater and more immediate return for a relatively smaller investment of energy." [5] Thus, Miller concedes that lower-class boys may on occasion behave legally, *but* only if they wish smaller and less immediate returns for greater investments of energy. As the smart youth who are reared in the lower class would surely know, there is little percentage in that.[6]

Richard Cloward and Lloyd Ohlin are the third of the contemporary depictors of the delinquent subculture. They clearly repudiate the radical separatism posited by Miller. However, their picture of the delinquent as committed to subcultural precepts is otherwise similar to Miller's and Cohen's portrayal. Cloward and Ohlin suggest that "Every culture provides its members with appropriate beliefs, values and norms to carry out required activities" and that "this is equally true of the subculture." [7] They disavow the radical separation between middle and lower class by insisting that the subculture "Is distinguished by the prefix 'sub' . . . to focus attention on its connection with a larger environing culture from which it has become partially differentiated." [8]

But after disavowing radical separation, their description of the relation between conventional culture and a variety of delinquent subcultures is basically similar to Cohen's. Delinquent subcultures are related to conventional culture through their *opposition*. They do not become related through reaction formation, as in Cohen's theory, but rather through alienation from conventional precepts and the availability in lower-class areas of an oppositionist view. Whatever the underlying reason, reaction formation, autonomous traditions, or alienation and availability, the relation between delinquent subculture and conventional culture is the same in the theories of Cohen, Miller, and Ohlin and Cloward. It stands in *opposition* to the conventions of middle-class morality and inexorably leads its adherents to the breaking of laws.

The members of a subculture of delinquency must break laws, not by definition but by hypothesizing that their subculture is a delinquent subculture. This theory of the relationship between a delinquent subculture and conventional culture is not without an element of plausibility since there are or have been authentically oppositional subcultures, and delinquents do after all violate one of the most important expressions of conventional culture—the law. Moreover, the unwritten character of the subculture of delinquency has meant that there is little direct access to its ideology as in case, say, of the radical or bohemian tradition. Thus, we have been free to infer subculture from action, and the temptation to equate the two has been almost irresistible, especially since it is the misbehavior that initially prompts attention to an otherwise inglorious tradition.

The values and norms implicit in the subculture of delinquency are obviously related to delinquencies, and these values and norms obviously depart in some manner from conventional traditions. However, the relation between the subculture of delinquency and the wider culture cannot be neatly summarized in the term opposition. The relation is subtle, complex, and sometimes devious. A subculture is almost always not simply oppositional precisely because it exists within a wider cultural milieu which affects it and which it, in turn, affects. Sometimes, it is true, the insulation and enmity is so great as to fundamentally divide the society. The result is a dualistic society such as colonial nations, or certain types of multireligious societies. On occasion the result is civil war. But can the subculture of delinquency be oppositional? I think not for two reasons. The subculture of delinquency is manned after all by children, and it would be surprising if this fact did not have some effect on the shape of the ideology. Children have a curious way of being influenced by the society of elders which frequently includes parents, almost all of whom, whatever their own proclivities, are united in their denunciation of delinquent deeds. Moreover, the character of the backdrop—conventional culture—is not as simple as usually depicted. Conventional culture does not consist simply of ascetic puritanism, middle-class morality, or the boy-scout oath. The conventional culture is complex and many-sided, including a wide variety of interrelated traditions. Once our conception of the subculture of delinquency is modified by the realization that its adherents are children, and our conception of the wider culture is modified by the realization that it is many-sided, the relation between the two may be seen in the rich complexity it fully deserves; now mindless of each other, or autonomous, now oppositional, now symbiotic, now parallel.

It may appear that the delinquents I have in mind are simply a different sort than those dealt with by Ohlin and Cloward. I think not, even though it can be granted that *very few* delinquents are committed to their misdeeds. But Ohlin and Cloward purport to describe the subcultural delinquents of slum life, a numerous and not a trivial lot. Cloward and Ohlin would not necessarily describe as subculturally delinquent "a group that tolerated or practiced these behaviors unless they were the central activity around which the group was organized." [9] Thus, a group that belongs to the delinquent subculture is "one in which certain forms of delinquent activity are essential requirements for the performance of the dominant roles supported by the subculture." [10] The fact that Ohlin and Cloward have in mind the garden variety of slum delinquent and not some esoteric exception can only be indirectly inferred since they never specify the ordinary or extraordinary character of their delinquents. That they have in mind the traditional sociological delinquent of slum life is evident because of their brief description of the sort of delinquent acts which do *not* depend on the prescriptions of a delinquent subculture. They exclude acts that are "secondary or incidental to the performance of essentially lawful roles." [11] Their example, fraternity pranks, is especially revealing of what they have in mind. Also excluded are the acts of neurotic and psychotic youngsters and perhaps lone offenders. Thus, it is evident that the issue is genuine rather than spurious. We have in mind the same referent, a subculture in which delinquency is intended and public, the most frequently described examples of which may be found in slum life. Since we are talking about much the same thing, the issue remains—the content of the subculture of delinquency. Does *that* subculture merely tolerate behavior, or "require it as a demonstration of eligibility for membership or leadership status." [12]

It may appear that in describing the delinquent subculture depicted by Cloward and Ohlin I have unfairly criticized the perhaps careless use of terms. But this is not so; Ohlin and Cloward mean precisely what they say. The delinquent must conform to the dictates of his world. "A member who refuses to perform further delinquencies must expect expulsion from the group." [13] One thing is wrong with such strong formulations: they are very likely misleading, at least in most instances. There is a wide variety of extenuating conditions, some usable only for specific exemption, some for a general exemption, which excuses members from delinquent activity. The extenuating circumstances that warrant exemption from participation in specific delinquent forays include, most revealingly, the admission that, "man, I'm not that bad." The key term "bad" is rendered with a double meaning, one the mundane, conventional meaning of bad, the other the esoteric, delinquent usage referring to a positively evaluated toughness. The double meaning reflects the underlying mixture of shame and pride with which the confession is made. The specific foray from which the member is granted exemption because of not being that bad depends on the stage already attained by him and his particular peer group. He may not be "bad" enough to use a gun, to commit a robbery, burglary, assault, or sometimes even to break curfew. The group may use persuasion or coercion, but it may also approve and indulge because its members are of two minds regarding their delinquencies. The two minds are well exemplified in their curious use of the term bad. Also among this class of extenuating circumstances are the normal excuses of children, ranging in credibility from headaches to house chores.

The extenuating conditions that warrant general exemption, *without expulsion,* include understandably the expectation of serious court sanction in the event of additional infraction, and less understandably such mundanely conventional things as part-time job after school or becoming involved with a girl friend. But, reply the theorists of the delinquent subculture, these simply indicate that the member is leaving the delinquent subculture, *by definition,* and that is the problem. They may win the argument easily, but the price they pay is tautological construction. If the issue is to be a real or empirical one, the question must be: can a member remain in the subculture of delinquency, the world of public delinquency, and through proper extenuation refrain from delinquencies. I suggest the answer is yes, and that the existence and the character of these extenuating circumstances inform us of the substance of the subculture of delinquency. They in-

dicate in a dramatic and forcible way the intrusion of conventional
values, and thus the accommodating rather than the oppositional
character of the subculture. But, counter the theorists of the delinquent subculture, even if the point is granted, are these not
by your own admission extenuating circumstances? Are they not
the exceptions that probe the rule? Is not the commitment to
delinquency *proven* by the fact that exemption is only granted
under extenuating circumstances? Ordinarily, the answer would
be yes, but not if delinquency is permitted only under certain
conditions, not if the subculture of delinquency approves only
of delinquency in the presence of other extenuating circumstances.
If some precepts that make up the subculture of delinquency grant
permission to perform misdeeds under widely available extenuating circumstances and if others grant exemption from the necessity of so behaving under widely available extenuating circumstances, where is the commitment? The subculture of delinquency,
I propose to suggest, is a delicately balanced set of precepts doubly
dependent on extenuating circumstances. Both the commission
of delinquent acts and abstinence from them are approved only
under certain conditions.

How can we tell if the subculture of delinquency is a delinquent subculture? One way is to assess the posture of delinquents
in a variety of circumstances. Recall, my thesis is that the subculture is of two minds regarding delinquency, one that allows members to behave illegally and to gain prestige therefrom, the other
reveals the impact of conventional precepts. Both frames of mind
are necessary if we are to accurately portray the subculture of
delinquency.

The Situation of Apprehension

If the subculture of delinquency were committed to delinquency, there would be little shame or guilt felt upon apprehension. When persons who are adherents of an oppositional subculture are apprehended by the agents of the dominant order,
they react with indignation, a sense of martyrdom, and fear of
the consequences of their apprehension. They do not, if they are
committed to opposition, ponder the righteousness of their deeds.[14]
Contrasted with the indignant righteousness of the opposition is
the shrug of the professional criminal or espionage agent who

views apprehension as a risk of his enterprise. Different from both is the response of the juvenile delinquent. Delinquents do frequently voice indignation in the situation of apprehension, but mainly because they believe or pretend to believe themselves unjustly accused. Unlike the adherent of an oppositional subculture, they agree that someone should be apprehended and punished, but it ought to have been someone else. Indignation may also be voiced concurrent with confession since the delinquent may claim that "others get away with it." Thus, the indignation of the delinquent differs from that of, say, a nationalist rebel. The delinquent's is a *wrongful* indignation.

Once the delinquent has expressed his wrongful indignation, he proceeds to either contriteness or defensive explanations. The contriteness that he manifests may be based on guilt, or more likely shame, but it cannot be dismissed as simply a manipulative tactic designed to appease those in authority. Much of the evidence that the expression of contriteness is not simply tactical is, to be sure, of a clinical nature or based on the impressions of those who deal with the offender. Thus, it must be used with caution,[15] but it cannot be ignored if we are to avoid the gross stereotype of the delinquent as a hardened gangster in miniature.

Many delinquents do not manifest contriteness and probably they do not experience it. Instead, they may justify their act but in a characteristically revealing way. Generally, behavior may be justified radically or apologetically. Radical justification asserts the righteousness of an act in and of itself. A wide assortment of behavior has been justified in this way ranging from the radical homosexual's assertion that love of men is an indication of higher sensibility to the assassin's belief in the righteousness of regicide. Note, however, that the same acts, homosexuality and political assassination, are capable of justification that is rendered apologetically. The homosexual apologist bases his plea for tolerance on the claim that inverts are driven to their unhappy circumstances by forces beyond their control. The apologist of *attentat* may justify it even though he grants it abhorrence. It may be the "only way" given the tyranny of the regime or the backwardness of the masses. The apologist deems the behavior necessary or provoked; it is unavoidable. But he evaluates the extraordinary act in terms of ordinary conventions. In a word, he *excuses* it.

Radical justification is characteristic of oppositional subcultures, whereas apology characterizes more accommodating subcultures. Some, like the subculture of homosexuals, are obviously mixed, with radical and apologist factions. However, the subculture of delinquents does not have such factions. With the exception of a few bizarre oddities who are regarded by ordinary delinquents as crazy, radical defenses do not appear. Instead, delinquents who are not given to contrite appearance justify their behavior through apology. Their slogans of justification include "No one gives you anything. Take what you can get," "There's no place to go or nothin' to do 'round here. What do you expect us to do with our time?," "I had to join that gang and use a knife. A guy has to defend himself, don't he?" His very slogans reveal his assessment of delinquency. It is necessary or unavoidable, but he evaluates it in terms of ordinary conventions. He excuses himself, but his gruff manner has obscured the fundamental sense in which he begs our pardon.

The Situation of Imputation

A boy in Bedford-Stuyvesant, a high-delinquency area in New York, was told by a companion that his brother is in jail. He beat his companion with an ashcan cover, denying the allegation. Years later, analyzing his motives, he said, "I felt no disgrace over having a brother in jail. I knew plenty of families who had a member locked up. Still I would not stand for anybody sounding me on it. Not even if what they said was true. That's the way we are down our way." [16] This is a typical situation of imputation, and I take the response described to be typical of delinquent drift. The boy says that "he felt no disgrace over having a brother in jail," and it is this claim that has been taken at face value and placed near the heart of the contemporary sociological picture of delinquency. The claim is heard many times, particularly in the situation of interview which for some sociologists is the only situation of relevance. But when placed in a situation of imputation, the claim that he felt no disgrace obviously cannot be taken at face value. The truth of the claim is somewhat suspect because of his peculiar use of the ashcan cover, his denial of the allegation that his brother was in jail, and, most important, his description of his companion's statement as "sounding."

Sounding is a key term in the vocabulary of delinquents, referring to perhaps the most frequent class of events in day-to-day mundane behavior of delinquents. Used properly, an analysis of sounding may be a choice instrument in an understanding of delinquent values. Like most terms in the delinquent part of the world, it has a double meaning, one conventional, the other esoteric. The conventional meaning refers to the plumbing of depth —a probing of how deep the façade of personal appearance goes —and by gradual adaptation a testing of one's status. The esoteric meaning of sounding is of more immediate relevance. It refers to the primary means through which status is probed—insult. What is insult? Insult is an imputation of *negative* characteristics. Offense is taken only if the recipient at least partially concurs with the perpetrator on the negative evaluation of the substance of the remark. We may not insult people for the possession of qualities they wholly celebrate.

Boys who live in the subculture of delinquency may be sounded because their brothers are in jail. Moreover, they may be and are sounded on the grounds of being bad or mean. "Man, you are a pretty bad (or mean) character, ain't you?" is the method of sounding a peer who claims to have attained an advanced stage of delinquency. Being bad is simultaneously honorific and grounds for insult.[17]

Delinquents take offense if they are falsely accused. Partially this is because they wish to prevent the punitive action which ordinarily follows accusation, but also because they concur in the conventional assessment of delinquency.[18] The imputation of delinquency is not only denied, which would happen in any event merely for truth's sake, it is also resented. If the subculture of delinquency were committed to delinquency, if it were oppositional, then imputations of delinquency might be true or false but in any case complimentary and hardly capable of eliciting resentment.

The delinquent especially resents the imputation of misdeeds to the significant others of his immediate familial environment. He is greatly concerned with the defense of reputation of pious mother, chaste sister, or conscientious brother or father. There is little of the out and out rejection of the law-abiding implied by the precepts of a delinquent subculture. The authentically honest are respected, often revered. Wrath is reserved for the pretender or hypocrite, and condescension for the "square."

The Choice of Victims

A common situation of delinquents is that of selecting victims. Though there is a degree of randomness in this choice, it is not wholly so because there are some conspicuous exemptions. Certain persons and institutions are exempt. This does not mean that they are never victimized. Delinquents violate the precepts of their subculture as well as those of the wider culture. But it means that there is a class of unapproved victims. Forays against such victims take place but they are not publicized. They are private, and thus beyond the limits of the subculture of delinquency whose defining characteristic is publicity. If they are discovered by adherents, if they accidentally attain publicity, response will range from mild to severe sanction. An example of mild sanction is sounding, and, curiously enough, an example of severe sanction is expulsion.

Who may claim exemption? There is considerable variation according to specific delinquent act, but generally the likelihood of exemption increases with proximity to the delinquent peer group. Most generally exempted are family and peers. All other exemptions seem idiosyncratic, held by some groups and not by others. Some groups may refrain from committing vandalism against the church of their own faith, or even churches generally. Others may not with approval roll drunkards of similar ethnic background.[19] Others may respect the feeble and the infirm.

Exemption of the family and peers from the pool of victims is not easy to maintain. The exemption of peers is particularly troublesome, partially because violations of family exemption are less likely to attain publicity than the victimizing of peers. The victimizing of peers (i.e., comrades in the same coterie within the delinquent subculture), especially in the form of theft and assault, occurs frequently despite the disapproval it incurs. This disunity of theory and practice is a potent source of rivalry, bickering, jealousy, and unstable cliques. It is one reason many juveniles leave the subculture the moment an attractive alternative arises

This tension-ridden state is more or less normal. It arises primarily from the double and conflicting consequences of proximity. In precept, proximity particularly in the form of membership entitles the card carrier to exemption from being seriously victimized, but in practice the chances of being victimized depend also on sheer availability, which in so provincial a world as that inhabited by delinquents puts a penalty on proximity. Fortunately, their world is not so provincial as to exclude neighborhood boys who do not subscribe to the subculture and who are not on other grounds exempt.[20] Also available are unexempted adults, and their property, consisting mostly of the unknown or disliked. And finally, there are the favorite targets, consisting of likeminded but separate coteries of delinquents. These are especially desirable for assault, but also, to the extent that they possess collective or personal property, for vandalism, burglary, and robbery.

What does the delinquent's intricate choice of victims reveal about the nature of his enterprise? It suggests that according to precept considerably different quotas of victims are drawn from favored and unfavored categories. In most quota systems prizes are awarded to favored categories and penalties to the unfavored. The concept of prize, and also of penalty, denotes a consensus between the donor and beneficiary. Exemption from being victimized is the prize doled out by the delinquent donors to the happy beneficiaries. Thus, on this score—in this situation as in others—there is consensus between delinquents and others. The thesis of the delinquent subculture may be reduced to absurdity by the proper insistence that if delinquents were dedicated to their misdeeds, they would victimize favored categories and exempt the unfavored. The thesis is not so absurd because the situation in question is only one. In some situations, as I have granted, the delinquent does act as if he were dedicated to delinquencies. But in many others, he reveals his conventional frame of mind.

The Juvenile Situation

Childhood, used broadly to include adolescence, is a position in a social structure, and as such possesses general qualities that shape and limit the possibilities of incumbents. Thus, to know that a person occupies the position child immediately tells us more than a little about what he is and is not able to do. Some elements of position inform us definitively—for instance, children may not vote, they may not with impunity be workers rather than students, and they may not without special dispensation be heads of families; other elements inform us not definitively but prob-abilistically, and it is this latter class on which I wish to focus.

Elements of the childhood position in American life make im-plausible the kind of delinquent subculture described by other writers. These elements do not make such a subculture impossible, but improbable. What are these elements and why do they reduce the plausibility of an oppositional subculture?

Juveniles are encircled by the members of adult society. Oppo-sitional subcultures may arise, but they are almost always in-sulated from the rest of the society. Ideally such subcultures consist of families rather than individuals; at the very least, indi-vidual emissaries receive nurture and support from the families they represent. Oppositional subcultures are further insulated by a network of special and appropriately censored media of com-munication, special schools, churches, voluntary associations, sum-mer camps, and neighborhoods. Thus, the network of multiple affiliations conspires to preclude doubt and optimize certainty and commitment. Such ghettoes need not be oppositional—often they are not—but an oppositional subculture flourishes under sectarian conditions. Once the sectarian conditions break down, the prob-ability of doubt, opportunism, and defection is heightened.

Now this formulation surely does not always hold; exceptions may be found, but usually not on a point so close to the opposite end of the spectrum. The conditions just described are ideal for the persistence of an oppositional subculture. If they are not necessary, they are at least facilitating. At the opposite end of the spectrum are the conditions of permeation and exposure. These include persistent contact with members of conventional culture, exposure to conventional schools, voluntary associations, summer camps, mass media, and residence in neighborhoods that are liberally infiltrated with conventional agents. Because of an over-whelming identification with the peer group, the delinquent possibly may remain unaffected by his situation of *encirclement,* but this is not probable. Once the belief in the existence of parental Fagins is surrendered, the whole idea of an oppositional subculture manned by children becomes dubious. And when we augment parents with all of the other agents of convention, the idea becomes implausible. Try as they do, the possibility of anything more than partial insulation is remote for all but a very few delinquents. The subculture of delinquency does reflect the partial insulation from conventional agents. But the same subculture also reflects the permeation of conventional agents resulting from the juvenile's predicament of encirclement.

A special word about parents seems warranted. The theory of a delinquent subculture makes no special note of family instability or severe intergenerational conflict. If anything, this theory prides itself in presenting at least on this count a rather normal child. The *bête noire,* to the extent that there is one, tends to be a school system that unwittingly rigs status contests in favor of the privileged, disappoints ambitious slum boys, or is simply mindless of the existence of the lower-class values. The family, which is put in its place by Cohen, has in the latest rendition, by Ohlin and Cloward, just about vanished from the slum area.[21] Even Walter Miller, who perceives the family, discusses it, and uses its peculiar structure to partially explain the shape and content of the delinquent subculture, fails to explain why it makes no conventional impact.

What sorts of relations do parents have with their delinquent sons? There is obviously great variation, but whatever the parental posture conducive to delinquency, it is not likely to be explicitly encouraging.[22] Parental Fagins are so rare as to be unimportant. Since parents normally function as agents of conventional culture, any breach in their relations with sons facilitates the possibility of the partial insulation required by a subculture of delinquency. But even a breach of relations does not liquidate parents, except in extreme instances, and thus the insulation is rarely more than partial. Parents have a way of intruding on the existence of children, even delinquent ones. Thus, the juvenile situation, too, indicates a subculture of delinquency that stands between convention and crime, committed to neither, influenced by both. I do not mean that there is a conventional and a delinquent subculture which individual juveniles accommodate in determinate ways; rather that the subculture of delinquency itself is a synthesis between convention and crime, and that the behavior of many juveniles, some more than others, is influenced but not constrained by it.

The Situation of Interview

Some sociologists, in practice if not theory, award a special place to one particular kind of social situation. Given the general sociological theory that individual behavior varies considerably according to role and thus situation, the tacit awarding of special place seems both gratuitous and curious. Even more curious, however, is the particular situation given such prominence—a situation in which a stranger asks an informant intimate and perhaps impertinent questions. What is the meaning of response to so peculiar a situation? The only plausible answer is that the meaning of the response depends on a host of factors including culturally variable attitudes to such interrogation and the extent to which the questioner can reduce the sense of estrangement and, instead, convey a sense of rapport. Also axiomatic is the fact that response to *this* situation must be augmented by responses to a wide variety of others. If the interview makes a plausible claim that these three conditions—a receptive cultural attitude to discussion of the topic in question, the illusion of rapport, and the augmenting of interview by a variety of other social situations—have been satisfactorily met, then its relevance may be granted. Once granted, its utility is based on the view that an aspect of self is revealed in the presence of a strange questioner who conveys a sense of rapport; not so outlandish a view if we surrender the tacit belief that special or crucial aspects of self are revealed. Aspects of self, each important in their place, are revealed in every social situation. Thus, the very peculiarity of the situation of interview may elicit aspects not amenable elsewhere.

The issue is whether the subculture of delinquency, as exemplified by the multitude of delinquents, is committed to delinquency or is ambivalent with regard to convention and crime; whether it is an oppositional or a compromise subculture; whether its justification of delinquency is radical or apologetic. The situation of interview is one in which the issue is resolved by some manner of question which is put to the delinquent. The issue may be disguised or relatively patent. The question put to the one hundred delinquents at a training school for boys was direct and simple.[23]

Each respondent was shown a series of pictures, each picture portraying a different offense. They were asked in a general way how they would feel about a boy who committed the particular offense being shown. The question was further clarified by adding, "Would you want to hang around with him or like him, more, less, the same, or what?" It was reiterated that their honest response would be appreciated. The question as posed might seem loaded, but I think not. I can think of no better way of translating the postulate of the delinquent subculture to adolescent boys than the statement that, other things unknown, they would respond favorably to a picture of boys committing presumably valued behavior.

The response to the situation of interveiw confirms the impression conveyed in the variety of situations thus far discussed. Adherents of the subculture of delinquency seem little committed to the misdeeds inherent in it. Just as important as the overall impression is the distribution of judgments. Approval and disapproval closely reflect the relative seriousness of the infraction.

DISTRIBUTION OF JUDGMENTS

Offense	Approve	Indifferent	Mild Disapproval	Indignation	N
Mugging	2	12	39	47	100
Fighting with a weapon	1	21	38	40	100
Armed robbery	2	22	27	49	100
Auto theft	2	46	22	30	100
Stealing from a warehouse	3	48	32	17	100
Stealing from a car	1	51	29	19	100
Vandalism	1	58	30	11	100
Stealing a bike	4	60	22	14	100
Total	16 (2%)	318 (40%)	239 (30%)	227 (28%)	800

The first thing of note in the distribution of judgments is the tiny proportion who approved of the act by suggesting in some way that they would admire, or like, or feel an affinity with the boy in the picture. The proportion is so small that little relation appears between the assessment of seriousness and the granting of approval—probably because of the small number of cases, but possibly because these are neurotic responses elicited by irrational associations. Thus, there are virtually no cases in which positive approval accrues to the perpetrator of these delinquent acts. Two per cent of the eight hundred judgments rendered by one hundred boys elicited positive approval. Of the sixteen approvals, nine were of the four least serious acts and seven of the four most serious.

The overwhelming majority of responses ranged from indifference to indignation. In total, 40 per cent of the judgments expressed indifference. ("It wouldn't make me no difference." "I could hang out with him or not." "If I liked him or not wouldn't depend on that.") Thirty per cent expressed mild disapproval. ("Man, that cat think he's bad. I don't go for that." "No, I don't like that kind of stuff." "I ain't that bad." "I keep away from cats like that, they get you in trouble.") Twenty-eight per cent responded with what could only be described as righteous indignation. ("I hate guys that do that." "That's a mean thing to do, he ought to be in jail for doing something that bad." "Guys like that are always messing things for everyone else; they ought to be put away.") The reader must be reminded that in not a few instances these were acts that had been committed by the respondent, so two-minded are the adherents of the subculture of delinquency.

Was I being misled? I believe not. Recall my thesis is that the subculture of delinquency entertains the commission of delinquencies under widely available extenuating conditions, but it does not commit adherents to their misdeeds. I shall attempt to elaborate this view in the following chapters. For the present it is enough to observe that the character and distribution of judgments in the situation of interview is totally consistent with the picture of drift and markedly inconsistent with the thesis of a delinquent subculture.

The Situation of Company

The final situation in which I wish to view the delinquent is one on which previous observers have almost completely focused.

It is the situation in which the delinquent is among his peers committing delinquencies, exaggerating, recounting, or planning them. It is a view of delinquents within their primary group context. I call it the situation of company. It is of course a most relevant situation, especially for the sociologist. However, professional loyalties notwithstanding, it is just another situation whose relevance must be considered and assessed, not simply declared. The situation of company is not the only reality. It is not the only situation in which we may catch glimpses of the self-expression of subcultural adherents.[24]

Thus, it could be granted without substantially detracting from my thesis that in the situation of company, the delinquent reveals himself to be an adherent of a delinquent subculture—a committed member of an oppositional viewpoint which he radically justifies. That would be the simplest way of dispensing with the situation of company, but because it is too simple, because it too forcefully posits the possibility of self-inconsistency, a more complicated view seems warranted.[25]

Men do not act similarly in all situations. They perform distinct roles in which they as actors are metaphorically different persons. Actually, however, they are the same persons, which suggests that some variable amount of integration among roles occurs. Among the factors limiting the amount of possible inconsistency is the insulation between various roles enacted by the self. If workmates and family members are wholly insulated one from the other, the possibility of persistent inconsistency exists. The possibility of inconsistency is considerably reduced if distance and insulation among roles is slight. The delinquent, primarily because he is a juvenile but also because of the provinciality of his subculture, exists within a narrow life space centering around a local turf which includes school, family, and peers.[26] Obviously, he manages some inconsistency. Consequently, he comes closer to being an oppositional delinquent in the situation of company than in other situations, but even there he does not quite make it.

A distinctive feature of the subculture of delinquency is that its beliefs are imbedded in action. This is partially true of all traditions but never as much so as in delinquency. We speak of the delinquent code as if it existed somewhere clearly displayed.

There are such patent codes in modern society. Their hallmark is that they are written. The code of delinquency is relatively latent. It is not written, except by sociologists, nor is it even well verbalized. Delinquency is well characterized as a relatively inarticulate oral tradition. Its precepts are neither codified nor formally transmitted. Rather, they are inferred from action which obviously includes speech. An ideology of delinquency in the sense of a coherent viewpoint is implicit in delinquent action, but this ideology is not known to delinquents. They are not conscious of an ideology because they have not bothered to work it out. Thus, they infer ideology from each other. This is the primary relevance of the situation of company. It is that context in which the subculture of delinquency is mutually inferred. Mutal inference is accomplished through concrete verbal directives, hints, sentiments, gestures, and activities. But as long as the subculture is inferred, it is not taught in the usual sense of the term. Instead, it is cued.[27] Each member of the company infers the subculture from the cues of others. The company is in a state of acute mutual dependence since there is no coherent ideology which may be consulted. There are only specific and concrete slogans. But there is no explicit general theory.

The mutual inference is a delinquent subculture. Each member believes that others are committed to their delinquencies. But what about each member, what does he believe of himself? Has he not revealed in a variety of other situations that he is not so committed? Possibly, he is transformed in the situation of company to a committed delinquent by dint of the cues he has received from others. Possibly, however, each member believes himself to be an exception in the company of committed delinquents. The intricate system of cues may be miscues. Since the subculture must be constructed from the situation of company, it may be misconstructed. But is this not implausible? All that would be necessary to straighten out the mess would be a discussion. The company consists of friends, and surely if delinquency is public, attitudes toward it could similarly become part of the common knowledge. But that does not necessarily follow. In every public, there is the realm of privacy. There are things that are not openly discussed, and thus do not become part of the common knowledge.

Frequently, the basis of privacy is *status anxiety*.[28] As such, it may preface a system of shared misunderstanding.

Status anxiety is not likely to attain publicity. Its distinctive feature is that the dissipation of anxiety may occur only through reassurance from those parties whose perceived rebuff initiated anxiety. The anxiety is about status, about how one *stands* within a specific or general company. A person suffering such anxiety may either put the question—how do I stand with you?—or, anticipating rebuff, he may indefinitely postpone it, in which case the anxiety is never dissipated, but instead is expressed in one way or another. Why does the delinquent suffer status anxiety, of what sort, and why does he not put the question?

The situation of delinquent company elicits two related anxieties. One reason for both may be found in an innocent pastime— sounding. Sounding is a daily and almost incessant activity of the delinquent company. But because of its mundane and legal quality, its effects have remained unconsidered. Sounding reflects the delinquent's status anxieties, and it aggravates them by minimizing the likelihood that they will be publicized and thus dissipated.

Sounding, it will be recalled, is a probing of one's depth, taking the form of insult. One's depth is never definitively certified. It is sounded almost daily. One's depth is probed along a number of dimensions, but two loom most important. Most sounding is a probing of one's manliness and one's membership. Are you really a man, or just a kid? Are you really one of us, or just faking it? Thus, each delinquent in the situation of company suffers generally from masculinity anxiety and specifically from membership anxiety. He can hardly avoid these anxieties. He is sounded daily by a jury of peers. Note, there is initially nothing different about the substance of delinquent anxiety. Most boys suffer some degree of masculinity and membership anxiety. But sounding which may or may not reflect greater initial anxiety eventuates in either case in an increase in the level of anxiety. Note, also, that the consequence of masculinity and membership anxiety is not delinquency, but only the prevention of publicity regarding the evaluation of delinquent acts. The function of anxiety is the limitation of discussion and common knowledge. Thus, it is a key fact in the emergence of the possibility of mutual misconception culminating in a system of shared misunderstanding. Each thinks others are committed to delinquency.

Why are the questions of masculinity and membership not put? And assuming my answer to be plausible, why does it follow that the question of delinquency is not put? The questions of membership and masculinity are not put because given the history of sounding one can anticipate the following kinds of responses: "Do I really like you? Yea, come here and suck and I'll show you how much I like you." "Are you really a man? Well, I don't know, man; sometimes I think you a kid and sometimes you a fag." The anticipation of these sorts of response makes good sense since one excellent way of temporarily alleviating one's own anxiety is the invidious derogation of others. Sounding is both a source of anxiety and a vehicle by which it may be temporarily alleviated.

The question of evaluation of delinquency is not put because it is almost immediately translated into a question of masculinity or membership. "Do I think that stealing a car is a good thing? Man, you a fag or something? Ain't you one of the boys?" The serious discussion of sentiments regarding delinquency is prevented by frivolous replies whose motive is a demonstration of depth and thus a suggestion that a formal sounding is unnecessary. Thus, the delinquent in the situation of company *does not consider* his misdeeds. Instead, he infers the assessments of others from barbed remarks whose basic motive is not an exposition of the subculture but an alleviation of status anxiety. Whatever the motive, however, the function of such remarks is to mislead the delinquent into believing that his subculture is committed to delinquency.

Is the delinquent forever trapped in this comedy of errors? I think not. Moreover, I believe that the ways out may be taken as partial confirmation of what surely seems a strange and implausible hypothesis. Recall my earlier point that the majority of delinquents do not become adult criminals. Among the manifold and complex reasons for the drift out of delinquency is one that is immediately pertinent. The serious evaluation of delinquency does attain publicity but not in the situations of company thus far described. There are two situations of company, one crescive and mundane, the other contrived and esoteric in which the public evaluation of delinquency may occur. Publicity and its implicit potential for correcting possible misconceptions and misunderstandings is commonly a preface to the drift out of delinquency.

The occasion for crescive and mundane publicity is friendship ideally involving two buddies. Why two? Sounding is a public display of feud. Since the couple is friendly they are not given to feuding except for appearance sake. When they are alone there is no wider company before whom to perform. Public evaluation of delinquency is possible in the situation of isolated couples. Though possible, it is not probable until the anxieties which soundings reflect as well as aggravate subside.

Masculinity anxiety is somewhat reduced when someone becomes a man rather than being a mere aspirant. Boys are less driven to prove manhood unconventionally through deeds or misdeeds when with the passing of time they may effortlessly exhibit the conventional signposts of manhood—physical appearance, the completion of school, job, marriage, and perhaps even children. Adulthood may not in all social circles definitively prove manhood, but it is always good *prima facie* evidence. In a revealing reversal, the incumbent of manhood may exempt himself from the demand to engage in delinquencies emanating from mere aspirants by condescendingly observing that it is, after all, kid stuff. This applies not only to rumbling but also to many forms of theft.

The reduction of membership anxiety is coincident with that of masculinity anxiety. The approach of adulthood is marked by the addition of new affiliations. One is less anxious about membership in the company of peers because there are new alternative affiliations. There were always alternatives but the new ones are more tenable since they are adult. They cannot be slandered as kid stuff and thus dismissed. Work, marriage, and other conventional adult statuses may be considered stupid or "square" but they are obviously not kid stuff. To that extent they invite affiliation. Their very existence serves to reduce the membership anxiety inherent in the subculture of juvenile delinquency.

Thus, the approach of adulthood converts the possibility of public evaluation of delinquency to a probability. In the majority of cases, pairs of delinquents discover one after the other that they had shared misunderstandings. They had not really been committed to delinquency—it was fun and each thought that others demanded it, but *they* had never really believed in it.[29] However, this does not always happen. A very small proportion may discover that they are in fact committed to their misdeeds. These *decide* to be criminals. A larger proportion never publicly evaluate delinquency and continue through adult life guided by their misconception of the subculture deriving from the system of shared misunderstandings. Each is privately uncommitted but publicly a receiver and transmitter of miscues suggesting commitment. Why does this group maintain its pluralistic ignorance?

There are many contingencies, but the pertinent factors are inherent in the conditions of publicity already described. They are merely the reverse side of the conditions converting the possibility of publicity to a probability: the frequency and intensity of the coupled relationship and the level of status anxiety. It is not the fact of coupling that is crucial but what can be said about delinquency. Everyone or almost everyone in the subculture of delinquency has a close buddy at one time or another. However, friendship varies according to intimacy and frequency. Thus, disliked adherents who less frequently enter into close coupled relationships are less likely than others to discover their misconception regarding the subculture of delinquency. But even if one is liked and thus involved in a series of close coupled relationships, the level of status anxiety sets limits on what may be discussed. Normally, the level of both status anxieties is reduced with the approach of adulthood. Sometimes, however, the membership anxiety remains high because the additional affiliations ordinarily inherent in adulthood do not occur. For a variety of reasons some members do not join a woman in marriage; others, and frequently the same members, do not join the labor force. Thus, the membership anxiety persists.

What of masculinity anxiety? Did I not suggest that the approach of adulthood is *prima facie* evidence of masculinity? Ordinarily, this is so but occasionally an additional and weighty piece of evidence may offset whatever reassurance of manhood one may find in the approach of adulthood. Often, the dwindling remnants of the old gang affiliate with younger cohorts. Obviously, this is quite functional in the transmission of the subculture. But what of its effect on the bearded adolescent? The increment of assurance painfully gained through the slow passage of years is cruelly offset by the humiliation of hanging around with mere kids. The level of masculinity anxiety persists or is heightened.[30]

Thus, the persistence of misconceptions ideally depends on the interrelated circumstances of superficial friendship, abstinence from the affiliations of work and marriage, and a chronologic descent into the still densely populated cohorts of the subculture of delinquency. Those who never discover their misconception become criminals, but they never decide to do so. They simply continue the drift into adulthood.

The occasion for contrived and esoteric publicity is commonly called group therapy but more accurately termed guided group interaction.[31] Public evaluation of delinquency may occur in guided group interaction, either in a street or institutional setting. Guided group interaction is pertinent because it may help confirm the initially implausible thesis of shared misunderstandings. The limited success of this technique may derive from the discovery of misconception during the many hours of public discussion. Given this interpretation, it is not insight into self that is the critical contribution of guided group interaction; rather, the discovery of the outlook of others.

The two settings of guided group interaction have offsetting advantages and disadvantages that set limits on its effectiveness. In the institutional setting, two possible ways of interpreting the discovery that others share one's private outlook may interfere with applying the knowledge gained. The participant may feel that his companions in therapy are simply responding in tactical fashion to the situation of incarceration. According to reports on guided group interaction, this feeling is dispelled in the initial stages of the process. These reports are credible if we assume the initially implausible assertion that delinquents are involved in a system of shared misunderstanding in which commitment to delinquency is a common misunderstanding. The reports on the dissipation of doubt are less credible, perhaps incredible, if we assume the initially plausible assertion that delinquents are committed to their misdeeds. Being more gullible about reported observations than speculative theory, but also for self-serving reasons, I prefer to assume that the reports on the dissipation of doubt are credible.

But even if the delinquent surrenders the belief that the outlook on delinquency expressed by institutional companions is a tactical response to the situation of incarceration, he is still left with the possibility that his civilian peers are different. This is the fundamental limitation of guided group interaction in an institutional setting.[32] Unless the delinquent assumes the unity of subcultural delinquency—the essential similarity of delinquents throughout a large territory—he may not easily apply his institutional discovery to mates in civil society. He may assume the unity of subcultural delinquency, but that is a risky and not entirely warranted choice. The delinquent is not a trained theorist and the generalization implicit in such a notion may elude him. Moreover, an assumption of the unity of subcultural delinquency flies in the face of the well-known enmities that abound in his world. True, he is confused on the term unity and takes it to mean cooperation rather than like-mindedness. But such equivocation is the stuff of social misconception. Finally, he may be unwilling to hazard the application of his discovery when he returns to his civilian mates. Even if the unity of subcultural delinquency becomes explicit through guidance or intuition, it is, after all, just a theory. The delinquent is surely capable of that observation. He may not be willing to risk his status as man and member to test so undocumented a nation. Thus, the guided group interaction of institutional setting is fundamentally limited in the transfer of discoveries to civilian life.

Guided group interaction, less formal to be sure, may also occur on a street setting. Here, too, the public evaluation of delinquency is not the focused aim of gang work. Here, too, effort is dissipated in a hundred directions. But just as in the institutional setting, public evaluation of delinquency is an almost inevitable byproduct of the gang worker's larger enterprise.

The limitations inherent in the street setting are just the reverse of those in the institution. On the street, the limitation derives from the fact that this is *his* company of peers. The obstacle to the public evaluation of delinquency and the subsequent discovery of misconception—status anxiety regarding masculinity and membership—are all here despite the intervention of the street worker. It is the relative absence of masculinity but especially membership anxiety that makes the discovery of misconception easy and rapid in the institutional setting, but also helps account for the frequently premature prognosis of reformation. The situation of incarceration is not simply an extension of the situation of authentic company. Minimal masculinity is demonstrated but one may easily claim the desire to do quick time. Membership anxiety is even less warranted since this is not his company of peers. The pace and ease of attaining public evaluation and the discovery of previously shared misunderstandings is slow and uncertain in the street setting. More of one's investments are here. That is the fundamental disadvantage of the street setting. Its advantage is obvious. Accomplishment of publicity, discovery, and the drift out of delinquency when attained are of more durable consequence than in the institutional setting.

In summary, my thesis is that even in the situation of company, commitment to delinquency is a misconception—first of delinquents and later of the sociologists who study them. Instead, there is a system of shared misunderstandings, based on miscues, which leads delinquents to believe that all others situated in their company are committed to their misdeeds. Thus, the situation of company perhaps does not result in a posture toward delinquency radically different from that revealed in the situations previously discussed. If in all situations the delinquent reveals a basic ambivalence toward his behavior, a new conception of his subculture may be warranted.

The Subculture of Delinquency: An Alternative View

The subculture of delinquency consists of precepts and customs that are delicately balanced between convention and crime. The subculture posits objectives that may be attained through delinquency but also by other means. Its customs allow delinquency and even suggest it, but delinquency is neither demanded nor necessarily considered a preferred path. The norms and sentiments of the subculture are beliefs that function as the *extenuating conditions* under which delinquency is permissible.

The subculture of delinquency is one of many. It shares with other subcultures certain general characteristics. Foremost among these general characteristics is some degree of differentiation from the parent culture and some degree of provisional utility or function. Subcultures are not the same as parent culture, and they are not without social use.[33] Beyond this, however, each subculture has special characteristics that reflect its constituency and its position in society. The special characteristic of the subculture of delinquency which is of critical relevance is the fact that it is manned by juveniles who, because of their station, are encircled by the conventional order. Their subculture is subjected to persistent infiltration by agents of convention and persistent modification by the canons of convention. The subculture of delinquency is dependent on and integrated with the conventional order more than most others.[34] Thus, the key to the analysis of the subculture of delinquency may be found in its considerable integration into the wider society and not in its slight differentiation. Two ideas express the main mechanisms of integration.

Neutralization

The explanation of something should first be sought at its own level. To do otherwise is to prematurely succumb to reductionism. Delinquency is an infraction of law. Thus, its explanation may be sought at the level of legal phenomenon and interpretation.[35]

Norms may be violated without surrendering allegiance to them. The directives to action implicit in norms may be avoided intermittently rather than frontally assaulted. They may be evaded rather than radically rejected. Norms, especially legal norms, may be neutralized. Criminal law is especially susceptible of neutralization because the conditions of applicability, and thus inapplicability, are explicitly stated. Most if not all norms in society are conditional. Rarely, if ever, are they categorically imperative. However, most norms, due to lesser codification and lesser rationalization, are stated generally. Exemptions from the directives implicit in them are claimed but ordinarily in ad hoc fashion. The exemption is defended by an appeal to a vague presumption of consensus. "I believe in church-going but on this particular Sunday, I was under the weather. Thus, I did not go. I beg your pardon." Should pardon be granted? We do not know, not even in principle because the conditions of applicability and thus inapplicability are nowhere clearly specified. Because in law the conditions are specified, neutralization is not only possible, it is invited. The criminal law, more so than any comparable system of norms, acknowledges and states the principled grounds under which an actor may claim exemption. The law contains the seeds of its own neutralization. Though there is dispute and argument with regard to particulars, the general principles of mitigation and negation of crimes are granted in law.

Ordinarily, delinquents do not know the law even though they often pretend to knowledge. Thus, there is no intent of suggesting that delinquents seize upon the loopholes provided and exploit them. They may try, but that is not the idea of neutralization. Instead, the idea of neutralization suggests that modern legal systems recognize the conditions under which misdeeds may not be penally sanctioned, and that these conditions may be unwittingly duplicated, distorted, and extended in customary beliefs.

The law is not opposed at the substantive level of prohibited action. With peripheral exceptions which are endlessly paraded by the exponents of relativism, everyone in our society and perhaps in all societies agrees that violations of personal and property rights, the substantive heart of the criminal law, are *sometimes* worthy of prohibition, notice, and arrest. The question is *when,* or under what conditions, and it is at that level that dissent appears. Previous theories of the delinquent subculture have mistakenly assumed that dissent, or opposition, occurs at the superficial, substantive level, at the level of what ought to be prohibited.[36]

Thus, dissent appears, but at an obscure level. The minimal directives to action that are implicit in legal prohibitions are neutralized below the surface. But curiously, even in dissent, there is considerable similarity between the conventional and delinquent view of when the law should be invoked. Despite the worthiness of its prohibitions, the law ought to be invoked less often, according to the delinquent view. The subcultural delinquent unwittingly extends the conditions of inapplicability considerably beyond the point conceded in law, but in so doing he extends them along the same general lines already indicated in legal principles. The delinquent's extension and thus neutralization proceed along the lines of the negation of responsibility, the sense of injustice, the assertion of tort, and the primacy of custom.[37] This coincidence of concern, the obscured similarity between conventional and deviant viewpoints, is the second general idea underlying my thesis of the subculture of delinquency.

Subterranean Convergence

Beneath the surface difference lies an obscured similarity. Sometimes this is so, often it is not. These obscure similarities are worth pursuing because without them we can hardly understand the persistence of so tenuous and precarious a system as the subculture of delinquency. The continued existence of the subculture is facilitated and perhaps even dependent on support and reinforcement from conventional sources. The subculture is buttressed by beliefs that flourish in influential sectors of the normative order. These views, which include the professional ideology of criminology, psychiatry, and social work, an emergent ideology of leisure, a celebration of the primitive in Bohemia and anthropology, the cult of cowboy masculinity in the mass media, and the persistence of provincial sentiments in insulated sections of metropolis, all reflect at critical points precepts in the subculture of delinquency. But we cannot point to these obscure but consequential similarities unless we first discontinue the current sociological practice of confusing a richly pluralistic American normative system with a simple puritanism. Puritanism or its routinized equivalent, middle-class morality, is one tradition among many in American life. No one has documented its continued dominance. *Les bourgeoises* have undergone such steady and militant attack since an allegedly grubby ascent to power that the persistence of their moral dominance would be quite surprising, except perhaps in the suburbs of Boston. The morality of the historical bourgeoisie has undergone drastic modification. Moreover, it has encountered moral rivals in the spirit of modern corporate enterprise, the influence of intellectuals in an increasingly educated society, and in the rise of specialized professions of welfare. Moreover, its ancient rival, the sentiments of feudal provincialism, was never more than partially vanquished. Unless the proliferation of important moral traditions in a pluralistic America is understood and granted, the sustenance of the subculture of delinquency by conventional beliefs in implausible.

To be consequential, the new traditions and the very old must be in the moral atmosphere of society. They need not reach the adherents of subcultural delinquency in pure and sophisticated form to support and reinforce it. On the contrary, the function of reinforcement and sustenance is best served if these beliefs are grossly vulgarized. But to be consequential, they must in some form be heard by members of the subculture.

The subculture of delinquency receives cultural support from conventional traditions. Moreover, it receives considerable social and personal reinforcement if we conceive of support as a range rather than an attribute. Thus, an apparently tenuous and precarious subculture delicately balanced between crime and convention has an additional source of stability. It is itself a subterranean tradition in American life.

A subterranean tradition is characterized by contemporary adherents linked to the past through local legacies and to the wider social structure by a range of support. It is an ideal case of an integrated subculture. Thus, it is an advancing of the fundamental sociological notion of the *relation* between society and its deviants.

The major contribution of sociology to the understanding of deviance has consisted of two fundamental insights. First, persistent deviance typically is not a solitary enterprise; rather, it best flourishes when it receives group support. Second, deviance typically is not an individual or group innovation; rather, it has a history in particular locales. Thus, according to the sociological view, the deviant is linked to society in minimal form through companies of deviants and through local traditions. When these minimal links appear we speak of a deviant subculture. The view of sociology is extended if additionally we explore the relations between that subculture and the wider cultural system. That extension is the essence of the idea of subterranean analysis. Such analysis requires the exploration of *connections* between localized deviant traditions and the variety of traditions in conventional society. Moreover, subterranean analysis implies an ongoing dialectic among a variety of conventional and deviant viewpoints, and that in the process of exchange each of the traditions is simultaneously stabilized and modified. The paradox of simultaneous stability and modification is the fundamental meaning of cultural pluralism.

Theodore Lownik Library
Illinois Benedictine College
Lisle, Illinois 60532

Subterranean tradition may be defined by specification of key points along the range of support. It is deviant, which is to say that it is publicly denounced by authorized spokesmen. However, the tradition is viewed with ambivalence in the privacy of contemplation and in intimate publics by most conventional citizens. The spirit and substance of subterranean traditions are familiar and within limits tolerated by broad segments of the adult population. Adolescent immersion in the delinquent tradition, or flirtation with it, is a suitable subject of nostalgic reminiscence and recreation. So popular is the pastime that surviving puritans are sometimes forced to either falsify a biography or ludicrously confuse their innocent naughtiness with the precepts of a subculture which under proper conditions countenances murder. Among youth, conventional versions of subterranean traditions —reasonable facsimiles stripped of the more intolerable aspects —are experienced by broad segments of the population. Teenage culture consists of the frivolous and mindless pursuit of fun and thrill. The experiences encountered in this pursuit ordinarily include many of the juvenile status offenses. Its spirit is a modification of that implicit in the subculture of delinquency. Thus, teenage culture may be conceived as a conventional version, a reasonable facsimile, of subcultural delinquency. Finally, of course, subterranean traditions have bands of adherents. These adherents are the bona fide members of the subculture. They are the carriers of its theory and the perpetrators of its practice. It is to that theory and its effects on practice that I turn in the subsequent chapters.

NOTES

1. Albert Cohen and James F. Short, Jr., "Research in Delinquent Subcultures," *Journal of Social Issues,* Vol. XIV, No. 3, 1958, p. 21.
2. Albert Cohen, *Delinquent Boys,* Glencoe, Ill.: Free Press, 1955, pp. 28, 35, 67, 68, 129–131.
3. Walter Miller, "Lower Class Culture as a Generating Milieu of Gang Delinquency," *Journal of Social Issues,* Vol. XIV, No. 3, 1958, pp. 5–19. Also, William C. Kvaraceus and Walter Miller, *Delinquent Behavior, Culture and the Individual,* Washington, D. C.: National Education Association, 1959, Chaps. 3, 4, 6, 9, 10.

4. Walter Miller, "Lower Class Culture as a Generating Milieu of Gang Delinquency," *op. cit.*, p. 18.
5. *Ibid.*
6. Smartness is a focal concern of delinquents, according to Miller; *ibid.*, pp. 9–10.
7. Richard Cloward and Lloyd Ohlin, *Delinquency and Opportunity*, Glencoe, Ill.: Free Press, 1960, p. 13.
8. *Ibid.*
9. *Ibid.*, p. 7.
10. *Ibid.*
11. *Ibid.*
12. *Ibid.* The plural rendition of delinquent subcultures by Ohlin and Cloward is irrelevant to the immediate argument. My argument with them is more basic than that. It pertains to the degree and character of differentiation between the conventional culture and the subculture of delinquency rather than differentiation among delinquent subcultures.
13. *Ibid.*, p. 13.
14. Illustrations of oppositional subcultures include early Christians and more contemporary religious sects, nationalist movements in colonial areas, and perhaps extremist doctrinaire political parties
15. See, for instance, Fritz Redl and David Wineman, *Children Who Hate*, Glencoe, Ill.: Free Press, 1951.
16. Ira Freeman, *Out of the Burning: The Story of a Boy Gang Leader*, New York: Crown, 1960, p. 41.
17. An analogous situation in the conventional world of graded bureaucracies is the statement that someone has become a "big shot." The expression simultaneously bestows honor and heaps insult by imputing a too-assiduous ambition or a too-obsequious polishing of apples.
18. They take offense even when the accusation is in the form of an impertinent question as in the situation of interview, and there is no implication of punitive action.
19. See Thrasher's account of the Itschkies and the immunity from rolling enjoyed by Jewish drunkards, *The Gang*, Chicago: University of Chicago Press, 1927, p. 315.
20. Conventional neighborhood boys and girls who are exempted from the pool of victims include not only family members but also "good kids" who are somehow liked, perhaps because they are simply nice guys (or pretty girls). The notion that the alternative in slum neighborhoods is between joining the gang or being brutalized is a myth largely executed by delinquents and their unwitting professional agents.
21. See the critique of Ohlin and Cloward which elaborates on this point in David Bordua, "Delinquent Subcultures," *The Annals of the American Academy of Political and Social Science*, November 1961, pp. 133–134.
22. Fritz Redl in Helen L. Witmer and Ruth Kotinsky (editors), *New*

Perspectives for Research on Juvenile Delinquency, United States Children's Bureau, Washington, D. C.: Government Printing Office, 1956, p. 61.

23. I have no notion of the representativeness of the one hundred delinquents. No one else has either, since the question of representativeness cannot be posed until we know the character and shape of the universe from which the sample is drawn. We know little if anything concrete about that universe. Thus, the question of representativeness, with regard to delinquents, is legitimate but probably premature. The informants were the first hundred delinquents over twelve and under eighteen with IQs above seventy-five who entered the institution after a given date. They were typically interviewed about a month after they entered this institution. My position as a researcher with no institutional affiliation was well known among the boys by dint of the inmate grapevine.

24. Dennis Wrong, "The Oversocialized Conception of Man in Modern Sociology," *American Sociological Review*, April 1961, pp. 183–193.

25. Prescott Lecky, *Self-Consistency: A Theory of Personality*, New York: Island, 1945.

26. Warren Miller, *The Cool World*, Boston: Little, Brown, 1959.

27. Cohen, *Delinquent Boys, op. cit.*, pp. 59–62.

28. For a more extensive use of a conception of status anxiety with respect to politics, see the essays in Daniel Bell, *The New American Right*, New York: Criterion, 1955.

29. The couple is the ideal situation of publicity and discovery of misconception, but slightly larger cliques may also undergo this process.

30. Other patterns of accommodating to declining gang membership are well described in Ohlin and Cloward.

31. See, for instance, Lloyd McCorkle, Albert Elias, and F. Lovell Bixby, *The Highfield Story*, New York: Holt, 1958; and Lamar T. Empey and Jerome Rabow, "The Provo Experiment in Delinquency Rehabilitation," *American Sociological Review*, October 1961, pp. 679–695.

32. A highly local institution which more or less coincides with the civilian street setting is limited because it quickly confronts the fundamental restriction of the street setting.

33. Cohen, *Delinquent Boys, op. cit.*, Chap. 2.

34. For a discussion of the integration of other youth subcultures, see my "Subterranean Traditions of Youth," *The Annals of The American Academy of Political and Social Science*, November 1961, pp. 102–118.

35. R. M. MacIver, *Social Causation*, Boston: Ginn, 1942, pp. 90–91; also, the work of Emile Durkheim, especially *Suicide*, Glencoe, Ill.: Free Press, 1951.

36. There is a limited sense in which these theories are correct. Some dissension exists regarding the legitimacy of a variety of peripheral offenses. Two classes of offenses are marked by dispute. One is the category of victimless offenses—mostly vice, and the other with which it overlaps, the status offense—acts prohibited only for incumbents of a specific

status. In our society most offenses of this sort apply to the juvenile status. However, theorists of a delinquent subculture definitely do not limit their argument to these peripheral offenses. According to them, the heart of the substantive code, assault and theft, is at issue, conventional persons concurring and delinquents dissenting from the legitimacy of current prohibitions. See Chapter 5.

37. The specific ways in which these principles underlying the applicability of criminal law are extended and the moral bind of law is neutralized are discussed in Chapters 3 through 5.

[3]

The Negation of Offense

THERE are millions of occasions during which a delinquency may be committed. Except for occasions covered by surveillance, virtually every moment experienced offers an opportunity for offense. Yet delinquency fails to occur during all but a tiny proportion of those moments.[1] During most of the subcultural delinquent's life he is distracted and restrained by convention from the commission of offenses. *Episodically,* he is released from the moral bind of conventional order. This temporary though recurrent release from the bind of convention has been taken for compulsion or commitment. It is, instead, almost the opposite. During release the delinquent is not constrained to commit offense; rather, he is free to drift into delinquency. Under the condition of widely available extenuating circumstance, the subcultural delinquent may choose to commit delinquencies. During most of his life, and for almost all of the lives of more conventional youth, he may not choose.[2]

The situation of unregulated choice is familiar to sociologists. It was the original meaning of "anomie." I refrain from using that term because of the many conflicting meanings it has acquired since Durkheim. I prefer the term drift partly to avoid the many implications of anomie but also to suggest the episodic rather than constant character of moral release. Thus, drift is episodic release from moral constraint.

Episodic release obviously does not fully explain the commission of offense. But it is a crucial part of the process culminating in delinquent action. There are other aspects of the process, but they cannot occur unless the moral bind has first been broken. During episodic release from moral constraint, one may commit delinquency. Intermittently, the nexus binding the self to legal

69

expectations is broken. The conditions of extenuation allow moral release. My thesis is that the normative precepts implicit in the subculture of delinquency are little more than a statement of these conditions. These conditions include the negation of offense, the sense of injustice, rudimentary conceptions of tort, and the primacy of custom. This chapter focuses on the negation of offense.

The commission of a legally prohibited act is not yet a crime. Crime has both a material and mental element. Legal convention asserts, and delinquents more than concur in the view, that overt action of itself may not be deemed criminal or delinquent. This holds for both juveniles and adults despite the far-reaching modifications occasioned by the rise of the juvenile court. Before the prohibited act is criminal, a missing element must be added. In law, the missing element is called *intent*. In the subculture of delinquency and in lay society, it is commonly called fault. All three, law, lay society, and subculture of delinquency, entertain the plea that "I was not at fault," but there consensus ends. The meaning of intent and the methods of documenting or construing it are different in each of the three realms.

Intent and the Juvenile Status

In advanced legal systems, liability to penal sanction and thus the designation of crime or delinquency, is limited. The conditions that limit liability "can best be expressed in negative form as excusing conditions." [3] These excusing conditions apply generally. The clearest exception to the rule may be found in crimes of strict liability. "These are for the most part petty offenses contravening statutes that require the maintenance of standards in the manufacture of goods sold for consumption; e.g., a statute forbidding the sale of adulterated milk." [4] Only seemingly ambiguous is the realm of juvenile offenses. Whatever the ambiguity of the juvenile code and its foundations, no juvenile court denies the relevance of intent. Indeed, the juvenile status itself is taken as a mitigation of the offense, thus justifying a specialized court with distinctive approach and philosophy. Thus, the defense to crime based on infancy is slightly extended to warrant special treatment of juveniles.

The general principle mitigating the criminal responsibility of children has ancient origins. As early as 1818 in the United States, the settled common-law doctrine was restated by Chief Justice Kilpatrick.

Since a child under seven "cannot have discretion to discern between good and evil" he is incapable of committing crime; between the ages of seven and 14 he is subject to a rebuttable presumption of incapacity; and after 14 he is presumptively capable.[5]

The common law was extended and modified in the enactment of juvenile courts, first in Cook County, Illinois, in 1899, and subsequently in comparable form throughout the nation.

The juvenile court's departure from strict adherence to due process has been upheld on the grounds that it is a civil court which dispenses protective care to its wards rather than penal sanction to criminals. Thus, it might appear that the notion of intent has little bearing in courts dealing with juveniles. Such a view would be completely misleading. The juvenile court dispenses penal sanctions, whatever it chooses to call them, and to that extent it is clearly concerned with whether the offender manifested intent. The concern with intent may be observed in ordinary proceedings of juvenile court despite the fact that it is often sloppily constructed and despite the fact that higher courts give the court considerable discretion in this matter as in others.[6]

To do otherwise, to display an indifference to the question of intent, would be a violation of common social and legal expectations regarding the necessity of a mental element in offense. Sometimes the juvenile court does not carefully consider the question of intent, but on those occasions it prepares the ground for yet another source of neutralization. When the juvenile claims to be without fault, when "he did not mean it," and when the court is indifferent to the issue, he senses injustice.[7]

The juvenile court masquerades as a civil court despite its telltale dealings in penal sanction. Even among its many proponents the disguise of civil court is rather a joke—one that is beginning to wear thin.

In the area of the child's constitutional rights the last decade has seen a minor but interesting revolt on the part of some highly distinguished judges. So repellant were some of the juvenile court practices that the judges were moved to repudiate the widely held majority rule that a delinquency hearing in juvenile court is a civil, not a criminal action. . . . This doctrine appeared so distasteful to a California appellate court that the following language appears in the opinion: "While the juvenile court law provides that adjudication of a minor to be a ward of the court should not be deemed to be a conviction of crime, nevertheless, for all practical purposes, this is a legal fiction, presenting a challenge to credulity and doing violence to reason." [8]

Thus, the relevance of intent in courts dealing with juveniles is obscured—but only slightly. The limitation of criminal liability through a recognition of the mental element in crime—or delinquency—is by now so traditional, so firmly implanted in Western nations that a court manifesting indifference would be regarded as tyrannical. The legitimacy of such courts would be challenged.

Intent and the Common Sense

The popular acceptance of the necessity of a mental element in crime does not arise from a lay or delinquent imitation of legal precepts, more likely it is the other way around. "A relation between some mental element and punishment for a harmful act is almost as instinctive as the child's familiar exculpatory 'But I didn't mean to.'" [9] Though this statement must be qualified in order to purge the high sin of ethnocentrism, it more or less stands when limited to public sentiments in the democratic West.

Holmes suggests that criminal liability is founded on "blameworthiness," which is his rendition of *mens rea*. A denial of that foundation, he suggests, "would shock the moral sense of any civilized community." [10] The law bases *its* concern with the mental element on the common sense of civil society. Holmes correctly concludes that "a law which punished conduct which would not be blameworthy in the average member of the community would be too severe for the community to bear." [11]

The insistence that intent be apparent before the imputation of crime has deep sources in the Western legal tradition.[12] Important among these sources is the reluctance to impute criminality. It is after all a serious designation. "Felon," says Maitland, "is

as bad a word as you can give to man or thing." Compared to
Maitland's sensibility regarding the far-reaching social implications of such imputation, the presumably enlightened view of
the modern juvenile court seems an example of pious obtuseness.
In a high-court decision upholding the juvenile court's indifference
to due process, we are told that since the purpose of such courts is
not penal but protective, "no suggestion or taint of criminality
attaches to any finding of delinquency by a juvenile court." [13]
One can hardly resist observing that the classical law knew the
common sense far better than the favorite son of positive criminology—the juvenile court.

There is considerable dispute among legal scholars as to the
precise meaning of *mens rea* and the precise methods by which
intent may be determined.[14] However, one thing is clear. Compared to the view of subcultural delinquency, the legal view holds
man far more responsible for his action. He usually intends what
he does. "The scope of excusing conditions in the law is limited." [15]
Under proper circumstances, the law "recognizes good faith or
blameless intent as a defense, partial defense or an element to
be considered in the mitigation of punishment." [16] Thus, the
question of intent or its degree may be relevant in deciding
whether an act is a crime, the kind or degree of crime, and the
kind or degree of penal sanction.

The offenses of juveniles, to begin with, are mitigated though
not negated. A specialized court for juveniles *is* the mitigation.
Whether this is real or nominal mitigation is a matter currently at
issue. The issue turns on two questions. Does the indulgence of
the court in its sentencing outweigh the loss of protection inherent
in the relative absence of due process? [17] And, is the "protective
care" or "treatment" dispensed by the juvenile court a reality or
mystification?[18]

Before a crime may be legally imputed, there must be reasonable assurance that there is a causal nexus between a prohibited
act and a self.[19] That is one way of interpreting the meaning of
mens rea. In order to commit a crime, a person must be responsible. He must have discretion, and thus the capacity to do evil. If
his self has not caused the act, it is not a crime. What else, aside
from one's self, can cause an act? The answer makes sense only
if one appreciates that the legal essence of self is *will*. If a pro-

hibited act is caused by something besides one's will, then it has not been caused by the self. Thus, all other authorized causes of an act are reasonable defenses to crime. They are excusing conditions because the actor has not himself caused the act.

An act may be caused by things other than self. Some things, but by no means all, are authorized by law and thus may serve to extenuate the offense. The range of authorized causes other than self is in law limited and narrow. The range in the view of subcultural delinquency is considerably more inclusive. Thus, the delinquent may assert that "he did not mean it," the agent of law may retort that as far as it can see, "he did mean it."

The legal position is best rendered "you acted willfully" which, operationally, usually means that the act cannot reasonably be attributed to accident, self-defense, or insanity. Each of these defenses to crime is in turn narrowly defined. Each has a limited and fairly specific meaning. Neutralization of legal precepts depends partly on equivocation—the unwitting use of concepts in markedly different ways. The widely available excusing conditions under which infractions are permissible for the subcultural delinquent are expansions and distortions of the same conditions that excuse the accused in law.

The subculture of delinquency implicitly expands and modifies the mitigants of responsibility along the lines explicitly indicated in law. The parallel development does not typically result from a delinquent imitation of law; rather, it is almost the opposite. Legal reasoning with regard to intent reflects common social concerns. The law did not invent the concern with blameworthiness; it reflected, specified, and codified it. In the delinquent view, as in custom generally, the formulations have remained diffuse and expansive.

The major bases of negation and irresponsibility in law rest on self-defense, insanity, and accident; [20] so, too, in the subculture of delinquency. The restraint of law is episodically neutralized through an expansion of each extenuating circumstance beyond a point countenanced in law. Each point of law is extended and in that sense distorted.[21] Let us consider each major legal extenuation and observe its transformation as it appears among the precepts of subcultural delinquency.

Self-defense

The law and the subcultural delinquent concur in the belief that self-defense negates an offense. When each view is described we may observe the similarities and differences between them.

The legal view of self-defense as extenuation is not easy to summarize. There is some difference of opinion among legal spokesmen, mainly because of the inherent ambiguity of certain key terms. One can only point to certain general ideas which are sufficiently distinct from those of subcultural delinquency so as to render the ambiguities unimportant. The differences of opinion among legal spokesmen are dwarfed by the similarity when compared to the view of delinquents.

One major distinction between the legal and the delinquent view of self-defense lies in the way in which *offense* may be taken. The legal view guards against the possibility of giving moral approval to the defender's taking the offensive. In the delinquent view, taking the offensive is countenanced. In law, taking the offensive vitiates a defense to crime. The tenets of subcultural delinquency are more generous. They allow the defender great discretion, both in the extent to which he may outdo his provocateur and in the way in which he may respond to provocation.

Provocations, verbal or physical, need not be taken lightly; but neither must they be retaliated. The subcultural delinquent, as usual, has options which he may exercise. Depending on context and mood, his response to appellations like "chicken," "maricon," or "mother fucker" may be indifference, playful rebuttal, angry retaliation, threat of assault, or explosive violence. Similarly, his response to being struck or a threat thereof may include chickening out, running to get his boys, friendly jousting, angry jousting, or a sudden raising of the ante—flashing a weapon.

The idea that he must respond by retaliating because of compulsive aggressiveness or subcultural regulation is another of the current criminological fancies that may be dispelled by the most cursory observation of delinquents. Provocations need not be taken lightly, but they may be. In many circumstances one is entitled to take offense if he wishes to exercise that option. This does not mean, however, that the subculture of delinquency has no sense of proportion. The precepts of the subculture do not claim that a member may do anything he wishes just because someone called him a "punk." If a member attempts to murder someone for calling him a punk, his companions are likely to think that he has "heart." But they also will feel, like the rest of us, that he is "out of his fuck'n head."

Within limits, therefore, the subcultural delinquent is entitled to take the offensive. That is considerably more than the law allows. The law generally will not entertain any notion of proportionality or "getting even." Legal extenuation depends on the threat to person or property. The defender may only stand his ground. The offense cannot be legally negated by self-defense that is prompted by a desire to get things even again. The subcultural delinquent regards the legal notion as rather peculiar. It seems to him to smack of cowardice. And so it does. The trial judge generally stipulates that if the coward's path is available it should be taken.

It was the defendant's duty, if possible, to retreat and escape. A man . . . has no right to resort to force and violence against another, even when the danger is imminent, even where he has reasonable cause to believe that he is in danger, unless he has no reasonable safe means of escape and retreat. Before a man can use force and violence under the law for his own protection . . . he must be so situated, he must be in such a position that he cannot safely retreat.[22]

If retreat is possible, or if the police or citizenry are available, the coward's path is warranted. Thus, it follows that situations which lack the quality of spontaneity hardly qualify as suitable defenses to crime. Returning to the scene all but precludes the possibility of legal extenuation; but not so for the subcultural delinquent. The law ceases to bind him, it is episodically neutralized whenever ample provocation occurs. Faced with provocation, he may not only defend, he may take the offensive.

The delinquent differs from the legal view on three major points. The subculture of delinquency allows a rule of proportionality, and then some; allows the decision not to take the coward's path, although it also allows that path; allows a return to the scene of provocation and even for prearranged conflict.

The law, reflecting the common sense, has long manifested uneasiness about the coward's path. It is after all not a manly or even a wise thing to flee from one's assailant seeking a reluctant citizenry or eternally scarce police. Thus, the law allows the defender to stand his ground after more or less indicating his desire to seek assistance. Moreover, the law allows the defender to regard his home as a haven. Consequently, the trial judge's instructions just cited were erroneous according to Cardoza—not in principle but in that particular case. The instructions were erroneous because:

The homicide occurred in the defendant's dwelling. It is not now and never has been the law that a man assailed in his own dwelling is bound to retreat. If assailed there, he may stand his ground and resist the attack. He is under no duty to take to the fields and highways, a fugitive from his own home.[23]

The rule of the coward's path is thus qualified in law. It is not everywhere applicable and least of all on one's own home ground. The law reflects the common sense that cowardice is not everywhere warranted, and momentarily it appears that the qualification is capable of easy and gradual extension. But law, being more explicit and self-conscious than custom, may draw strict lines beyond which a qualification may not be extended. Custom is less exacting.

The law draws the line at the home—not an inch beyond. Cardoza, in the same reversal, approvingly cites *People v. Sullivan.*

The murdered man and the defendant lived in a boarding house. Their rooms were on different floors. The affray started in the defendant's room. The two men separated and the defendant's victim went downstairs. At the foot of the stairs he turned and went back. The defendant, instead of taking shelter in his own room, remained on the landing of the stairway. The fight was renewed and the murder followed.[24]

The crime in *People v. Sullivan* was not negated because the offensive was taken. The defendant was not at home. Instead he was on the stairway outside his room. The law purposefully restricts the area within which the rule of the coward's path is qualified. The specific demarcation is in some measure arbitrary.

The subculture of delinquency manifests concerns that are similar to those of law. Its conclusions are somewhat different from the legal view, but in some ways perhaps similar.

The coward's path is not unknown to the subcultural delinquent. He often takes it, especially when away from home. He calls his home "turf." But at home, on his turf, though he may take the coward's path, it is not well advised. He is especially reluctant to take the coward's path if the aggressor is an outside assailant. He is reluctant because on his turf he wishes to maintain a reputation as brave or courageous; but also because to flee from a haven in which there are dozens of unreluctant citizens eager to render assistance would not be a coward's but a fool's path. The basis for excepting home or turf from the general rules of behavior seems similar in both domains—legal and delinquent. This similarity partially confirms the notion that both reflect the common sense.

Why does the law exempt the home from the general prohibition against standing one's ground? Imputing motives to law is perilous, but nonetheless worth the risk. To require the coward's path when one is assailed at home is to commend the fool's path. The presumption is that home is safer than the "fields and highways." Moreover, to become a fugitive from one's home is to leave behind possessions and persons whose expropriation or assault may have been the assailant's motive for invasion. Thus, the coward's path is not required or even commended because it presumably leads to *greater*, and not lesser, danger of personal injury or financial loss than standing one's ground.

An additional motive may be imputed, though with less confidence. The law maintains great concern with the preservation of parental and especially paternal authority. The idea of the family as the fundamental social institution—the bulwark of order and stability—is no recent sociological discovery. Consequently, the law balks at commending the coward's path in the presence of wife and children. Parental order and stability is partially based on paternal reputation. Application of the rule of the coward's path would endanger that reputation. The rule has been stated in the following way:

Before a man can use force and violence under the law for his own protection . . . he must be so situated, he must be in such a position

that he cannot safely retreat. . . . We may not feel always like re-
treating in the face of an attack; it may not seem manly to us; but it
is the law that if a man can safely retreat . . . he must do so even
though it may not seem dignified and manly.[25]

The law excepts the home from that rule because it knows, it
shares in the common sense, that to demand of a man that he
behave in an undignified and unmanly way in the presence of
wife and children is to endanger the esteem and respect in which
he is held. The law cannot bring itself to so threaten the basis of
familial respect; so it modifies the rule of the coward's path. The
subcultural delinquent cannot bring himself to threaten the basis
of respect among his familial surrogates. Consequently, he too
makes special provision for his home ground, the turf.

The legal and delinquent views of self-defense are similar but
different. The legal view may be summarized in the following
directives: You must never take the offensive; in most situations
you must take the coward's path, if possible; at home, however,
you may stand your ground. The view of the subcultural delinquent may also be summarized: You may always take the offensive though not without some sense of proportion; ordinarily,
you may take the coward's path, stand your ground, or take the
offensive, basing your decision on a cool assessment of the situation; at home, however, you are ill advised to take the coward's
path.

Thus, whenever the delinquent is assailed or provoked, the
moral bind to law may be neutralized. He may in every situation,
on turf or off, take the offensive. Whether he does or not depends
on occasion and mood. The possibility of delinquency exists since
the compunction to conform emanating from the bind of law has
been neutralized. He may now drift into delinquency.

There is a special situation in which the delinquent's peculiar
view of self-defense serves as an extenuation of offense. The subcultural delinquent frequently engages in combat activities. His
conception of self-defense allows him to justify the existence of
a company of peers who, among other things, are given to intermittent conflict with other like-minded congeries. Combat, which
includes both guerilla attack and conventional battle, is a staple
of the subculture of delinquency. Though its frequency, form,
and virulence may vary by time and place, gang fighting has prob-

ably been a standard feature of the subculture since its emergence.[26]

The subculture of delinquency has persistently included among
its prominent activities periodic rivalries in which the use of
violence is countenanced. The most dramatic form of violence—
formal battle—is currently referred to as a "rumble." In earlier
times, these formal battles were called "rallies" or merely street
fights. More common and perhaps more dangerous, though less
dramatic than formal battle, is the guerilla foray into enemy
territory or the ambushing of interlopers who have wandered off
their own turf.

Combat is an activity, realized or potential, of all companies
within the subculture of delinquency. It is one of the standard
steps in the development of delinquency. Moreover, it is a standard expectation among delinquents that sooner or later they will
engage in some form of combat. Such combat is obviously illegal.
Moreover, battery, mayhem, murder, carrying deadly weapons
are offenses that lie at the heart and not the periphery of criminal
law. How is regular and anticipated participation in such activity
explicable without violating the picture of the delinquent thus
far developed?

The subcultural delinquent's conception of self-defense allows
him to engage in combat *justifiably*. The alleged motive for combat is always defensive, by no means an unusual fancy. Combat
is contemplated in the interests of self-protection or self-defense.[27]
Moreover, self-defense is interpreted generously and loosely to
finally countenance preventive action. Self-protection suggests the
protection of the company and its territorial prerogatives. Protection against actual attack suggests the defense of a company's
integrity against slurs on its honor and other forms of provocation.
Defense against explicit slurs suggests retaliation against sly
slurs implicit in the too-assiduous quest for "rep" on the part of
other companies. Thus, the delinquent conception of self-defense
is capable of considerable stretching. Like many customary and
unwritten precepts, it lacks the disciplined means of restricting
indefinite expansion. These means are implicit in codified and
rationalized systems like law.

A conception of self-defense that justifies preventive aggression
in anticipation of provocation is typically expedited by a sense
of history. The stretching of the concept of self-defense appears

considerably less illicit if one sees the situation in historical context. The history of combat between companies or their lineal predecessors is sufficiently rich, and the causes of previous combat sufficiently ambiguous, to provide ample justification for taking the offensive in the interests of defense. Thus, violent response to trivial provocation or even the initiation of aggression may qualify as negations of crime since the rival company may be accused of some symbolic or historic offense.

Because of the history of squabble and enmity among various delinquent companies, their territory warrants the description of tinderbox of metropolis. Offense may be taken at any point, and the peculiar conception of defensiveness allows the offensive to be taken. Whether it is or not, whether a formal battle occurs depends on a host of factors, only a few of which deserve mention. The likelihood of combat depends on the internal situation of the respective rivals, their relative power, the alliances they can muster, the availability of arbiters, and the effectiveness of police surveillance.

The moral bind of law is neutralized through the subcultural conception of self-defense. Thus, the company may drift into delinquency. But as usual, there is no assurance that the drift will culminate in actual delinquent behavior. Whether the rumble ever occurs or not depends on the aforementioned factors and numerous contingencies. But the crucial step has been taken. Through the agency of neutralization, the delinquent has been put in drift. He *may* commit delinquency. Over the long run, it is reasonable to expect that on occasion the drift will culminate in actual combat. But in any single instance it is difficult if not impossible to determine whether the loosening of social control implicit in drift will result in the commission of offense. The delinquent's subculture is simply too rich in options, too poorly delineated and specified, too ambivalent about its enterprises to yield anything approaching clear-cut directives to action.[28] There is an inescapable element of uncertainty in the enterprise of subcultural delinquency.

Insanity

The current legal view of insanity is in a confused state, and it is somewhat foolhardy to try making sense of it. Nevertheless, such an effort is necessary. Fundamentally, the legal view is marked by confusion because it has been unable to synthesize classical and positivist canons, and it cannot see its way to deciding between them. Synthesis of the two conceptions of man is logically difficult; choice between the two is empirically improbable. A diffuse legal conception of insanity is likely to persist, and thus a description of that view is subject to considerable controversy. Moreover, the distinction between the legal and delinquent conceptions of insanity remains blurred for much the same reason. Positivist and classical conceptions affect both the legal and the delinquent conception of insanity as a defense to crime.

Thomas Szasz points to one of the major sources of difficulty. The introduction of positivist reasoning in the form of psychiatric science has shifted the legal status of insanity. From the vantage point of law, "irresponsibility for a harmful act by reason of insanity . . . is entirely similar logically to irresponsibility for such an act because it happened accidentally or in self-defense." [29] The act is not criminal because the mental element is lacking. Extenuation is granted because the actor did not cause the act. Thus, the accused is released from legal responsibility. The statement that the actor did not cause the act makes sense given the classical assumptions of law. It makes considerably less sense, given the assumptions of positive criminology and its foremost court agent—modern psychiatry.

From the positivist perspective, an assertion that the actor did or did not cause the act simply makes no sense. It is either banal or false. Man's actions, criminal or conventional, are caused by antecedent events. The classic legal meaning of the statement is apparent. The actor's legal self—*will*—did not do it. As Szasz suggests, it is as if the act were committed by accident or for reasons of self-defense. It occurred through no *choice* and thus through no fault of the perpetrator. Moreover, the classic conception of insanity holds it to be a legal fact subject to the same canons of logic and evidence as self-defense or accident. The court was to reach a decision through testimony and examination as to whether the accused behaved willfully. It was to decide whether the actor possessed the legal aspect of self. Will, the legal aspect of self, has little relation to personality, the psychiatric aspect of self.

The psychiatric aspect of self—personality—and the related

concept of mental illness currently appear in court, and it is their presence that confuses the issue of insanity. The presence of psychiatrists, the ensuing confusion between will and personality and insanity and mental illness is apparent irrespective of whether Durham or M'Naghten rules. In both domains, expert testimony on whether an actor caused an act and is thus responsible is given by exponents of a modern scientific discipline that denies the fundamental premises on which their testimony is to be based. The spokesmen of enlightened modern psychiatry purport to have somehow remained insulated from the common sense which knows both choice and constraint, both responsibility and extenuation. It is this common sense that is the foundation of the legal conception of insanity.

The confusion that reigns in the current status of insanity is of note because the delinquent viewpoint flourishes when it receives sustenance from conventional sources. Unlike the legal system, the subculture of delinquency may have it both ways. The extension of the legal conception of insanity proceeds through capitalizing on the variety of available meanings. The laity which is the usual source of subterranean support is in this case augmented by elements from within the law itself.

The excusing of offense because of being "sick" or "mixed up" may seem reasonable and acceptable to influential elements ensconced in the administration of juvenile justice; more so, in fact, than it seems to the delinquent who himself asserts the extenuating claim. The idea of being sick or mixed up seems incongruous with the delinquent's traditional self-image of manly toughness and precocious independence. Because of the incongruity between the occasionally expressed excuse and the traditional self-conception of delinquents, we may suspect that this defense to crime—mental illness—probably had exogenous origins. Whereas most differences between the legal and the delinquent viewpoint seem based in the indigenous social circumstances of the subculture, the defense of mental illness was probably coopted by delinquents from court and welfare agents. When extenuating reasons are disseminated by conventional agents and incorporated into the subculture of delinquents, neutralization is likely to take on an especially tactical or Machiavellian character. Thus, this excuse does not have the authentic ring of many of the others.

When delinquents claim irresponsibility based on their peculiar conceptions of accident or self-defense, they do so plausibly. But when they justify their misdeeds on the basis of family troubles and other forms of adolescent unhappiness, they seem to reveal, perhaps purposefully, their disbelief and insincerity. Most seem unable to say that they are sick or mixed up without giving the impression that they are "putting you on." Irrespective of whether he believes himself to be sick, the subcultural delinquent would prefer that others did not believe that of him. Being sick, his rendition of mental illness, seems neither masculine nor adult. Thus, it is not likely to attain prominence in his milieu. But since this defense may be favored by many juvenile court agents, some delinquents make use of it.

The preference among delinquents is to expand the more traditional notion of insanity. "Going crazy" is somehow more manly than being sick, and thus the company of delinquents prefer that formulation and the extenuating circumstance implicit in it. "I lost my temper. I was crazy with anger." *Temporarily*, he did not know the nature of what he was doing. *Temporarily*, he could not distinguish between right and wrong. The italicized term distinguishes the delinquent view from the legal rule of M'Naghten.

Moreover, one may fall under the influence of external forces. Most prominent among these are alcohol and pharmaceutical stimulants. The law may sometimes allow being under the influence of alcohol to offset its assessment of specific intent but not general intent.[30] Not only is alcohol prohibited for minors, which is another matter altogether, but the law generally does not free persons from responsibility when they voluntarily engage in behavior which has foreseeably mischievous and dangerous consequences.[31] From the delinquent viewpoint, however, the offense is certainly mitigated and often negated. Being under the influence of alcohol is likened to losing one's mind, going crazy.[32]

When drift culminates so rapidly in a show of angry aggression or thoughtless expropriation, the act is likely to be viewed as an automatic pathologic response to a stimulus. However, the general pattern of neutralization and drift may be posited. The loss of temper or the state of inebriation episodically breaks the bond with moral order. The system of normative control temporarily loses its hold on the member of society. When the bind of law is neutralized, a drift into delinquency may occur. The only difference between this and other types of drift is the amount of time that passes between drift and possible culmination. There is an explosion. From the viewpoint of subcultural delinquency, the adherent has lost his mind, or at least misplaced it. He no longer acts willfully. Instead outside forces have taken control. Since he has been taken by a momentary insanity or an irresistible impulse, the subcultural delinquent sees himself as absolved of responsibility.

Accident

The subcultural delinquent's meaning of accident differs from the legal precept in two ways. One expands the legal meaning of accident, the other distorts it.

The law precludes *recklessness* from the category of accident.[33] The subcultural delinquent includes it. Recklessness is not a legal defense to crime because reasonable men grasp the foreseeable consequences of a particular line of action. Hitting a pedestrian is a foreseeable consequence of reckless driving. Similarly, doing injury to person or property is a foreseeable consequence of recklessly wielding a weapon. Beginning a line of action that foreseeably culminates in violation allows the construction of intent. However, law reveals its allowance for degree of intent by compromise. The lesser degree of guilt or use of less severe penal sanction reflects the difficulty with which intent is constructed. That the accused "did not mean it" matters, but not to the extent of fully excusing the foreseeable consequences of reckless behavior.

Thus, recklessness is neither accident, providing grounds for negation, nor completely intentional, providing no mitigation whatever. In addition to the compromise regarding the mental condition of the offender, the law uses a simpler expedient in resolving this obviously difficult issue. It relies on statutory innovation. Recklessness itself becomes an offense, especially when driving but also more generally. Reckless behavior goes under many names but most often is referred to as malicious mischief, incorrigibility, ungovernability, disturbing the peace, and even "juvenile delinquency." These categories of offense are all marked by a vagueness and inclarity unbecoming of law which generally prides itself on specificity and clarity. However, this is apparently the price one pays for resolving an inherently knotty issue by the expedient of statutory innovation. The ambiguity of recklessness cannot be removed since it is a mental condition, a state of mind, rather than an overt act. The ambiguity may only be transferred from the mental to what appears to be the material or substantive level.

Subcultural delinquents view the matter somewhat differently. Their dissent is partially principled, but also due to the intellectual shortcomings of a subculture manned by schoolboys. The logic of the legal view of recklessness which includes elements of compromise, subtlety, and sophistry is likely to elude the subcultural delinquent since he is completely untrained in such arts. Let me try to replicate what I take to be his train of thought.

An act either is intended or not. Recklessness is a state of mind which either implies intent or it does not. Clearly, I am reckless. I do not deny that. I did not bother to foresee the consequences of my line of action. But how could I? I am reckless. It's not a crime to be reckless. It's like being a wild kid.

Three points may be inferred from this reconstruction of the delinquent's argument. First, he has excluded the middle between intent and its absence. Second, in introjecting the properties associated with a term, recklessness, he has reified them and thus precluded the possibility of having behaved with care. Third, he has expressed a principled dissent with law at the substantive or material level. In so doing, he makes the transition from the first mode of legal response to recklessness, compromise, to the second, statutory innovation.

The subcultural reaction to statutory innovation is primarily one of withholding legitimacy. Whereas the delinquent consents to the central prohibitions in criminal law, he dissents from the propriety of many peripheral violations. The statutory innovations that pervade the juvenile code and prohibit various forms of "messing around" or precocious adult behavior do not elicit approval. In his reaction to these peripheral offenses, the subcultural delinquent looks rather like the portrait drawn of him in the theory of the delinquent subculture. But even with regard to peripheral offenses, the delinquent does not typically posit the rightness of the act; instead, he unwittingly incorporates and modifies yet another legal concept. He conceives of many peripheral offenses as torts—acts that are wrong and, if they lead to personal harm, warrant redress and compensation. But they are not deemed worthy of inclusion in the criminal law.[34] Moreover, the response to statutory innovation contains elements of indignation. Like the irate customer who is belatedly told about the fine print, the subcultural delinquent senses injustice. Since he is a major consumer of justice, his standards are quite high. Justice must not only proceed fairly and with great care, it must not be petty.[35]

By expanding the concept of accident to include recklessness, the delinquent widens the conditions under which offense may be negated. He may behave wildly and without due care regarding the foreseeable consequences of his behavior. Thus, he may on occasion drift into delinquency. Given his construction, he has not caused the act. It was accidental.

The subculture of delinquency not only expands the legal concept of accident, it distorts the concept. The offense may be negated and responsibility absolved through *accidents of circumstance*. As in the case of self-defense, concepts may be fundamentally modified through a sense of history. Defense of self may refer back to historic aggression by the enemy. Similarly, accident may refer to biographical events and not simply to those surrounding the offense. Accidents of circumstance refer to bad luck—antecedent events, natural and supernatural, which shape one's destiny.

According to the delinquent's subcultural precepts, bad luck is an extenuating condition and thus a defense to crime. A man's fortune is not his fault. Since man is not responsible for his fortune, he cannot be responsible for its unfolding.[36] Thus, intent, the mental element in crime, periodically vanishes. When it does, the moral bind is broken and one may drift into various forms of delinquency.

A belief in fate and destiny liquidates intent. Thus, in nations stressing the mental element in crime, like our own, such beliefs are fundamentally corrosive to legal order. If the belief were fully and always accepted, the restraint of law would be correspondingly fully and always neutralized. Fortunately, no one in our society (perhaps no one in any society) is fully given to the precepts of fate. The belief in the complete sway of destiny is precluded by the equally pervasive sense that man himself makes things happen. Man experiences himself as both cause and effect. Both are implicit in consciousness of self, and of the relation between one's self and one's surroundings. That we affect our surroundings and are affected by them is the common sense.

The delinquent is subject to frequent oscillation between sensing himself as cause—humanism—and seeing himself as effect—fatalism. Everyone experiences this oscillation. However, the delinquent may experience it somewhat more intensely because the precepts of his subculture are receptive to the older, traditional notions of fatalism. The subculture of delinquency may be seen as emerging at the crossroads between provincial and metropolitan life. Thus, it maintains the traditional belief in luck and destiny. But since it is an integral part of modern advanced society, the subculture of delinquency has incorporated humanistic elements. Consequently, the delinquent does not always conceive himself the victim of circumstances. He is not always irresponsible. Crime is extenuated and thus permissible only when he is reminded of destiny, when he recalls that he is controlled by external forces. This happens occasionally, and thus he is free to offend often enough to be the personification of the picture implicit in a notion of delinquent drift. He avoids, as does our picture of him, two extreme caricatures—the one arguing that he is no more delinquent than others, the other implying many more offenses than even he commits. He may drift into delinquency when he is in a fatalistic mood, when he is reminded of himself as effect.

What puts the delinquent in the mood of fatalism? What reminds him of fate? As so often happens, he gives us the answer but we fail to hear him. He is reminded of fate when, as he puts it, he is being "pushed around." To be "pushed around" is to be controlled by external forces. We fail to understand the import of this metaphor unless it is taken in a context of drift.

When we ask delinquents why they act as they do, and when their initial responses are probed, they frequently say that it was because of being "pushed around." The common reaction is to either take him at his word and sympathetically concur with him on a kind of naive frustration-aggression theory, or to reject his statement on good positivist grounds—he has failed to provide us with significant differences. Others get pushed around but only he and his companions persistently commit delinquency. That may be true, but it is misleading. The fatalistic mood, the sense of being pushed around, is only one bit of the process that includes everything thus far discussed—status anxiety magnified by the round of sounding, mistaking the content of his subculture, and the subcultural precepts regarding the conditions that extenuate offense. It makes little sense to take each element out of context, to gaze at it and to reject it because it does not significantly differentiate delinquents from other boys. That the subcultural delinquent is not significantly different from other boys is precisely the point. He is marginally different and only in process is there a cumulation sufficient to sometimes culminate in infraction.

Being "pushed around" puts the delinquent in a mood of fatalism. He experiences himself as effect. In that condition, he is rendered irresponsible. The sense of irresponsibility puts him in drift. Drift makes him available for delinquent acts. Whether the drift culminates in delinquency is up to him. Stripped of moral guidance, he momentarily exists in stark and frightening isolation. The precepts of his subculture episodically free him from moral restraint, but in so doing make him even more acutely dependent on the members of that subculture. He turns to peers to rescue him from drift. But that is not their function. Instead, they function to exacerbate his mood of fatalism and to provide the context of mutual misconception. Why does the situation of company exacerbate and often precipitate the mood of fatalism?

The situation of company could not remind a participant of destiny and thus liquidate responsibility unless the concept of accident of circumstance included natural as well as supernatural aspects. Strictly speaking, destiny refers to control by supernatural entities, and surely there is nothing supernatural about peers. But the subculture of delinquency expands the concept of destiny primarily through receipt of a handy assist from the naturalistic counterpart of fatalism—determinism. The subculture, which thrives on conventional sustenance, has incorporated the

modern canons of determinism into its traditional fatalistic framework. In so doing, it has of course vulgarized these canons. Thus,
supernatural destiny, which is taken only half seriously by subcultural delinquents, is augmented by natural determinants. The
two viewpoints are well blended. The important differences between them in the source, quality, and degree of constraint is
passed over. Unlike positive criminology, the distinction between
natural and supernatural determinants has made little impact on
the subculture of delinquency. But like the positive criminologist,
the classical humanistic assumptions of will and reason make no
impact on the delinquent—not when he is in the mood of fatalism.
In this mood, the subcultural delinquent looks as if the positivist
portrait of him is accurate. But it is not. The likeness is deceiving.
He is not constrained to commit delinquencies. He is free to
commit them.

Once the concept of destiny is enlarged, the situation of company may remind the delinquent of himself as effect. He is one
of many. He is in a state of acute dependency, especially if he
has been thrust into the hands of the company by a prior incident;
but the company itself may also elicit the mood of fatalism since
it too "pushes around" many of its members.

The situation of company may either exacerbate the fatalistic
mood or it may initiate it. The mood may also be initiated in another situation frequently experienced by children—encirclement.
The situation of encirclement, which is dominated by conventional
agents of adult society, frequently features the "pushing around"
of subordinates. Parents and officials, depending on the tactics
they use, sometimes behave in a manner that reminds the juvenile
of himself as effect. However, a simple command is not sufficient
to elicit so downcast and dangerous a mood. To be put in drift,
the delinquent must be jolted. His tenuous but nevertheless existent bind to society must be broken. To be reminded of destiny
is to temporarily quit society.

Subterranean Convergence

Under proper circumstances, the subcultural delinquent considers himself irresponsible. His self-conception is confirmed, perhaps surpassed, by views held in certain quarters of conventional

society. The delinquent's claims are perhaps surpassed because in certain conventional ideologies there is little compunction to make irresponsibility dependent on accident, self-defense, or insanity —even in their expanded delinquent form. According to certain spokesmen, we are all always irresponsible because our behavior is determined by natural events over which we do not exercise control. The subcultural delinquent is exposed to and hears— his ears are perked—pronouncements from a variety of allegedly reputable sources which confirm his viewpoint. He hears, distorts, and capitalizes on these pronouncements.

If I may anticipate, it will be charged that these conventional pronouncements and messages are taken out of context. They are. The views I shall describe are usually modified, complicated, and ratiocinated by the spokesmen who represent them. However, if our concern is with how delinquents hear these pronouncements, it helps to take them out of context, but not randomly. Instead, we should attempt to bend our reading of popular ideologies in the manner of the delinquent. We should model our style of misreading or misunderstanding along the lines of juveniles who, to begin with, lean toward or adhere to the precepts of subcultural delinquency. If the research in communication has taught us anything, it has alerted us to the considerable propensity of listeners to distort, to misinterpret, and generally to incorporate whatever they hear into already existent frames of reference.[37] My main purpose in pointing to conventional parallels of delinquent views is not to expose villains. Rather, it is to explore the reinforcement of subcultural precepts by conventional ideas. Because the subculture of delinquency is itself delicately and precariously balanced between crime and convention, it best achieves stability within a context of wider cultural reaffirmation.

Extreme and blatant affirmation of criminal irresponsibility has gone out of vogue. No longer may we directly witness the incredible spectacle of a Clarence Darrow addressing the prisoners in Cook County jail in 1902, informing them of their complete lack of responsibility.

The people here can no more help being here than the people outside can avoid being outside. I do not believe that people are in jail because they deserve to be. They are in jail simply because they cannot avoid it on account of circumstances which are entirely beyond their control and for which they are in no way responsible. . . . Many of you people are in jail because you have really committed burglary; many of you, because you have stolen something. In the meaning of the law, you have taken some other person's property. Some of you have entered a store and carried off a pair of shoes because you did not have the price. Possibly some of you have committed murder. I cannot tell what all of you did. There are a great many people who have done some of these things who really do not know themselves why they did them. I think I know why you did them—every one of you; you did these things because you were bound to do them. It looked to you at the time as if you had a chance to do them or not, as you saw fit; but still, after all, you had no choice. There may be people here who had some money in their pockets and who still went out and got some more money in a way society forbids. Now you may not yourselves see exactly why it was you did this thing, but if you look at the question deeply enough and carefully enough you will see that there were circumstances that drove you to do exactly the thing which you did. You could not help it any more than we outside can help taking the positions that we take.[38]

Modern proponents of such sentiments would hardly contemplate expressing such ideas in a speech to an audience of criminals; but not because such ideas do not exist. Such ideas have become partially institutionalized in the correctional establishment. Consequently, they are not romantically shouted from the rooftops. Such flaunting expression would be, as one perceptive prisoner in Darrow's audience commented, "too radical." Nowadays, such ideas are expressed at academic symposiums and in college textbooks. But their impact is not limited to intellectual audiences. The message of Darrow is persistently cued to delinquents as they interact with their professional caretakers.

Characteristically, the most extreme and thus the most useful pronouncements may be found among spokesmen for the psychoanalytic viewpoint. Occasionally, the delinquent's talent for distortion and vulgarization is hardly evoked. John Hospers, a modern philosophic determinist of psychoanalytic persuasion, states:

There are many actions . . . for which human beings in general and the courts in particular are inclined to hold the doer responsible, and for which I would say he should not be held responsible. The deed may be planned, it may be carried out in cold calculation, it may spring from the agent's character and be continuous with the rest of his behavior, and it may be . . . true that he could have done differently *if* he had wanted to; nonetheless, his behavior was brought about by the unconscious conflicts developed in infancy, over which he had no control and of which (without training in psychiatry) he does not have knowledge.[39]

Hospers' statement is unusual only in the clarity with which the point is made. His position is more or less shared by psychoanalysts and especially by their social-work entourage. In the event that the delinquent has difficulty in incorporating naturalistic psychic determinism into his traditional supernatural framework, people like Hospers do it for them.

Consider a spendthrift. . . . One will say that he could have overcome his spendthrift tendencies; some people do. Quite true: some people do. They are lucky. They have it in them to overcome early deficiencies by exerting great effort, and they are capable of exerting the effort. Some of us, luckier still, can overcome them with but little effort; and a few of us, the luckiest, haven't the deficiencies to overcome. It's all a matter of luck. The least lucky are those who can't overcome them even with great effort, and those who haven't the ability to exert the effort.[40]

Hospers may not be a sophisticated spokesman for the psychoanalytic position. I would imagine that he is not. But his statement is of value precisely for that reason. He has superbly rendered the position in precisely the simplified form heard by the delinquent. Moreover, he has supplied the link to a supernatural framework.

Hospers' statement is a radical defense of the thesis of psychic determinism. Most others of his persuasion would probably reject a statement so simple and so free of mystification. But is not his rendition the logical outcome of a hard determinist view? What is must be because it is. Even if one changes, it is because he had it in him to change. If he does not change, it is because he was unlucky.

The strange thing about hard determinism is its extreme gullibility. It is a "scientific" philosophy imbued with faith and given to utopian promise. No determinist claims that currently we know the causes of delinquency. A few grant that at least in the interim we must hold man responsible, but having said this they proceed to vitiate the concession by referring to it as a necessary fiction. However, Hospers and those who share his view are not compromisers. The promissory note must be immediately converted.

Let us suppose it were established that a man commits murder only if sometime during the previous week he has eaten a certain combination of foods—say, tuna fish salad at a meal also including peas, mushroom soup, and blueberry pie. What if we were to track down the factors common to all murders committed in this country during the last twenty years and found the factor present in all of them, and only in them? The example is empirically absurd; but may it not be that there is some combination of factors that regularly leads to homicide . . . ? When such factors are discovered, won't that make clear that it is foolish and pointless, as well as immoral, to hold human beings responsible for crimes? Or, if one prefers biological to psychological factors, suppose a neurologist is called in to testify at a murder trial and produces X-ray pictures of the brain of the criminal; anyone can see, he argues, that the *cella turcica* was already calcified at the age of nineteen; it should be a flexible bone, growing, enabling the gland to grow. All the defendant's disorders may have resulted from this early calcification. Now, this particular explanation may be empirically false; but who can say that no such factors, far more complex, to be sure, exist.[41]

It is a joy to behold a determinist who is direct, clear and uncompromising. Note the unfolding of his argument. The conjectural *if*, in the middle of a paragraph, is converted to a foreseeable *when* and the implications for policy are drawn *now*.

Many of the practitioners who directly confront the delinquent more or less share the views of Hospers. It is difficult to know how many. Those that do, however, are in no position to render their sentiments so radically. Instead, if the delinquent claims irresponsibility, they are likely to reply: "It is true that it is not really your fault, but still you have to accept responsibility for what you have done." The delinquent, untrained in sophistry, finds something unreasonable in that observation. He must choose between one clause or the other. One requires obliteration, the other commemoration. Which he obliterates and which he commemorates should by this time be obvious.

Does anyone ever say such things to delinquents? Yes, they do. I cannot say how often but I have heard statements like the one just cited made repeatedly in juvenile courts by judges and by social-work aides attached to the court. What is said privately to juveniles by psychiatrists, social workers, and even policemen probably surpasses what is publicly spoken. Modern guides written for those who work with juveniles stress the importance of supporting the child. Whenever supporting the child leads to statements excusing or understanding his behavior, as they occasionally must, the precepts of subcultural delinquency are also supported.

If the delinquent were constrained, either through compulsion or commitment, such statements would matter little if at all. But if he exercises choice, and if his subculture is merely an assertion of extenuating conditions, such statements are of consequence. They are part of the causal nexus culminating in delinquency in that they bolster an otherwise precarious and brittle system of beliefs. Statements reinforcing the delinquent's conception of irresponsibility are an integral part of an ideology of child welfare shared by social work, psychoanalysis, and criminology. This ideology presents a causal theory of delinquency which, when it attributes fault, directs it to parent, community, society, or even to the victims of crime.

The ideology of child welfare has gained considerable influence in schools, social agencies, and juvenile court. It is resisted in all three contexts and especially in the court. But even its opponents in juvenile court are forced to pay frequent lip service to it because only by repeated public reference to the ideology of child welfare have higher courts been able to countenance and justify the procedural laxity that characterizes such courts. Though the practice of the court is dominated by one or another form of penal sanction, or the postponement thereof (i.e., probation), its philosophy is that of child welfare and treatment.

Among the central tenets of this ideology is the attribution of fault to parents. This attribution is but a portion of a larger social rhetoric which views the family as *the* source of subsequent developments in the lives of children. There is obviously merit in such a contention but it is not without problems. A second faction within the child-welfare establishment senses the problems entailed in a notion of parental culpability. They keenly realize that parental failings, too, are determined, and thus parents are not responsible for their wayward youngsters. Consequently, they ask: what determines parental inadequacy? The typical answer is community or society. A few, possessed of a sense of history, say grandparents. Even fewer, possessed of great sophistication, suggest that among the many, many factors implicated are the victims themselves, who because of their own problems elicit or seduce the criminal act.

What is wrong with such formulations? Are they not the stuff of many textbooks in criminology and social work? There are three major problems with the view that holds the larger collectivity—parents, community, or society—responsible for the waywardness of an individual member. First, such formulations confuse the analytic concept of cause with the moral concept of fault. Second, even if one takes fault to be the moral analogue of cause, it is not clear why fault is best attributed to underlying rather than immediate agents. Third, if the attribution of fault to underlying agents is defensible, we should seriously dwell on the response of delinquents to the fact that *they* and not parents, neighbors, or citizenry receive correction through the medium of probation or incarceration.

The ideology of child welfare confuses the analytic concept, cause, with the moral concept, fault. The canons of cause and effect simply imply the creation of models specifying the conditions under which certain outcomes are probable or certain. Especially in sociology, but generally in all nonexperimental disciplines, there is no definitive specification of precipitants because each set of conditions may in turn be explained by another set. Consequently, depending on how one looks at it, there are always additional antecedent or intervening variables. One may always proceed further back in the pursuit of causes or fill in the gap between the conditions specified in the model and the predicted outcome. Thus, the causes are no freer than the outcomes. Both are the unfolding of personal, social, and cultural process. To equate fault with cause is to imagine that culprits have not themselves been victimized by yet another set of culprits. It is for this reason that the fault of parents is transferred to community, society, or history.

But may not one view fault as a moral analogue of cause? Probably yes, if we remember to put it the other way around. Historically, the analytic concept, cause was an anthropomorphism. It was an extension to the physical world of the human sense that we make things happen—the sense that we are responsible for events.[42] We make good things happen, in which case we are praiseworthy, and bad things, in which case we are at fault. Thus, the analogy between cause and fault is both historically and logically defensible. However, causal analysis in the social world offers little guidance as to how far to extend the causal chain. Thus, the fundamental question remains. At what point in the causal chain may we best attribute fault? Even if we accept the analogy, we get no closer to an answer. The attribution of fault remains a moral question with no definitive answer. It is surely far from clear that a sophisticated attribution of fault to underlying determinants has greater merit than a simple assignment of blame to the person who committed the offense. Both the underlying process and a willful self, as I shall elaborate later, are part of the causal chain culminating in the criminal act.

Whatever our philosophical preferences in the assignment of fault, the question of consistency—the avoidance of hypocrisy—is paramount. We may not without consequence assign fault to the larger collectivity and penal sanction to the individual member. The consequences of such discrepancies between theory and practice are heightened in institutions that require the consent of subordinates. The juvenile court is such an institution. The juvenile court requires a greater grant of legitimacy from its clientele than previous courts because its aspirations are loftier. It wishes to rehabilitate the accused, not simply to suppress or remove him. The capacity to accept treatment depends greatly on the trust accorded the court and its agents. Hypocrisy—saying one thing and doing another—is fundamentally corrosive of trust. To philosophically attribute fault to underlying conditions, but to actually hold the immediate agent responsible is an invitation to distrust. And to refer to penal sanction as protective care is to compound the distrust. Thus, by its insistence on a philosophy of child welfare and its addiction to word magic, the juvenile court systematically interferes with its alleged program. By its own hypocrisy, perceived and real, it prepares the way for the delinquent's withdrawal of legitimacy. Without the grant of legitimacy, the court's lofty aspirations cannot be effectively pursued.

Thus, the ideology of child welfare supports the delinquent's viewpoint in two ways. It confirms his conception of irresponsibility, and it feeds his sense of injustice. Both support the processes by which the moral bind of law is neutralized. Both facilitate the drift into delinquency.

NOTES

1. The incidence of delinquency among confirmed delinquents is very high compared to those that are officially known, but very low compared to opportune occasions. The first point is explicit and the second implicit in Fred J. Murphy, Mary M. Shirley, and Helen L. Witmer, "The Incidence of Hidden Delinquency," *American Journal of Orthopsychiatry*, October, 1946, pp. 686–696.

2. My purpose is to elaborate a view of delinquency that has been propounded frequently but always developed within a positivist framework. Recent statements of "social control" theories of delinquency appear in Albert J. Reiss, Jr., "Delinquency as a Failure of Personal and Social Controls," *American Sociological Review*, April, 1951, pp. 196–207; F. Ivan Nye, *Family Relationships and Delinquent Behavior*, New York: Wiley, 1958; Walter C. Reckless, *The Crime Problem*, New York: Appleton-Century-Crofts, 1961, Chap. 18.

3. H. L. A. Hart, "Legal Responsibility and Excuses," in Sidney Hook (editor), *Determinism and Freedom in the Age of Modern Science*, New York: Collier, 1961, p. 95.

4. *Ibid.*

5. *State v. Monohan*, In Richard C. Donnelly, Joseph Goldstein, and Richard D. Schwartz, *Criminal Law*, New York: Free Press of Glencoe, 1962, p. 855.

6. A substantial literature on the juvenile court, mostly critical, has appeared in recent years. See, for instance, *Comparative Survey of Juvenile Delinquency*, Part 1, New York: United Nations Department of Economic and Social Affairs, New York, 1958 (prepared by Paul Tappan); Francis A. Allen, "The Borderland of the Criminal Law," *Social Service Review*, June 1958, and "Criminal Justice, Legal Values and the Rehabilitative Idea," *Journal of Criminal Law, Criminology and Police Science*, September–October 1959; Margaret K. Rosenheim (editor), *Justice for the Child*, New York: Free Press of Glencoe, 1962; Lewis Diana, "The

Rights of Juvenile Delinquents: An Appraisal of Juvenile Court Procedures," *Journal of Criminal Law, Criminology and Police Science,* January–February 1957, pp. 561–569; Robert G. Caldwell, "The Juvenile Court: Its Development and Some Major Problems," *Journal of Criminal Law, Criminology and Police Science,* January–February 1961; Sol Rubin, *Crime and Juvenile Delinquency,* New York: Oceana, 1961, Chaps. 4–5.

7. A fuller discussion of the sense of injustice appears in Chapter 4.
8. Paul W. Alexander, "Constitutional Rights in the Juvenile Court," in Rosenheim, *op. cit.,* p. 83.
9. *Morisette v. U.S.,* in Donnelly, Goldstein, and Schwartz, *op. cit.,* p. 565.
10. Oliver Wendell Holmes, *The Common Law,* Boston: Little, Brown, 1946, p. 50.
11. Exception may be taken with this statement but only through a fundamental misinterpretation of its meaning. Holmes is not referring to the substantive law but rather to blameworthiness or *mens rea.* Thus, the claim that there are considerable differences among sections of a nation in their evaluation of specific law, say, with respect to the vices, may be true but it is irrelevant. Holmes' statement requires only one clarification. The assertion that civilized communities could not "bear" laws that ignored blameworthiness should not be taken to mean that such communities could not "survive" such laws; obviously, communities could and have, as witnessed in totalitarian societies. Many, though not all such communities, have survived the concept of "objective" enemy of the state which is an explicit repudiation of the mental element in crime. Citizens cannot "bear" such laws in the sense of not being able to "stomach" them—not being able to refrain from privately observing that such laws are unjust and tyrannical.
12. Paul Radin, "Criminal Intent," *Encyclopedia of Social Science,* Vol. 8. pp. 126–130.
13. In re Holmes, in Donnelly, Goldstein, and Schwartz, *op. cit.,* p. 272.
14. Here and throughout, the intricate and detailed aspects of legal opinion are avoided. Elementary and consensual aspects of law suffice in drawing the contrast with the precepts of subcultural delinquency. Consequently, I have been able to rely on introductory and authoritative statements of criminal law.
15. Hart, *op. cit.,* p. 99.
16. *Morisette v. U.S.,* in Donnelly, Goldstein, and Schwartz, op. cit., p. 569.
17. Rubin, *op. cit.,* Chap. 4.
18. Allen, "The Borderland of the Criminal Law," *op. cit.,* and "Criminal Justice, Legal Values and the Rehabilitative Ideal," *op. cit.*
19. R. M. MacIver, *Social Causation,* Boston: Ginn, 1942, Chap. 8.
20. Thomas Szasz, "Criminal Responsibility and Psychiatry," in Hans Toch (editor), *Legal and Criminal Psychology,* New York: Holt, Rinehart and Winston, 1961, p. 150.
21. The elliptical construction may be misleading. Thus, I reiterate. It is

not that delinquents and laymen know the law and carelessly bowdlerize it, but just the opposite. The law knows the common sense implicit in custom and carefully specifies it.

22. *People v. Tomlins,* in Donnelly, Goldstein, and Schwartz, *op. cit.,* p. 665.
23. *Ibid.*
24. *Ibid.*
25. *Ibid.*
26. Discussions of street and gang fighting may be found in Herbert Asbury, *The Gangs of New York,* New York: Knopf, 1928; Richard O'Connor, *Hell's Kitchen,* Philadelphia: Lippincott, 1958; and Lewis Yablonsky, *The Violent Gang,* New York: Free Press of Glencoe, 1962; for a view placing emphasis on temporal and social variation to the point of positing specialized combat and theft sub-subcultures, see Richard Cloward and Lloyd Ohlin, *Delinquency and Opportunity,* Glencoe, Ill.: Free Press, 1960.
27. This should not be taken to mean that in actuality there are not aggressor gangs and defensive gangs. There are, just as there are aggressor and defensive nations. Confusion is introduced and analysts are misled because the vocabulary of defensiveness has been coopted by aggressor gangs and nations.
28. For a discussion of the conversion of drift to actual infraction, see Chapter 6.
29. Szasz, *loc. cit.*
30. For a discussion of the legal view of intoxication as a defense to crime, see Herbert Wechsler, "On Culpability and Crime," *The Annals of the American Academy of Political and Social Science,* Vol. 339, January 1962, pp. 33–34.
31. *Ibid.*
32. The offense of using alcohol while still a minor is neutralized in another way which will be discussed in Chapter 5.
33. Wechsler, *op. cit.,* pp. 29–30.
34. This line of argument is more fully developed in Chapter 5.
35. See Chapter 4.
36. Walter Miller, *Delinquent Behavior: Culture and the Individual,* Washington, D. C.: National Education Association, 1959, p. 67.
37. For instance, see Eunice Cooper and Marie Jahoda, "The Evasion of Propaganda: How Prejudiced People Respond to Anti-Prejudice Propaganda," in Ralph Turner and Lewis Killian (editors), *Collective Behavior,* Englewood Cliffs, N.J.: Prentice-Hall, 1957.
38. Arthur Weinberg (editor), *Attorney for the Damned,* New York: Simon and Schuster, 1957, pp. 3 and 6.
39. John Hospers, "What Means This Freedom," in Hook, *op. cit.,* p. 126.
40. *Ibid.,* p. 137.
41. *Ibid.,* p. 132–133.
42. MacIver, *op. cit.,* pp. 35–37, 57–62.

[4]

The Sense of Injustice

THE major function of the subcultural views thus far described is to extend the area of personal irresponsibility. Given these views, delinquency is permissible when responsibility, the moral bind between the actor and legal norms, is neutralized. The sense of irresponsibility is the immediate condition of drift. Beneath the immediate condition is a state of readiness. The delinquent is prepared to convert irresponsibility to freedom from moral constraint because his subculture is pervaded by another and more profound condition of neutralization. This additional condition—a sense of injustice—does not ordinarily serve as an immediate condition of drift. Instead, it normally provides a simmering resentment—a setting of antagonism and antipathy—within which the variety of extenuating circumstances may abrogate the moral bind to law. Occasionally, however, a sufficient, profound sense of injustice may directly elicit the feeling of being pushed around and thus the mood of fatalism.

The subculture of delinquency is integrated into the wider cultural order, but in a tenuous way. It is partially incorporated and partially alienated. Ambivalence to law is one manifestation of its tenuous incorporation. As discussed in the previous chapter, this ambivalence is reflected in its basic agreement with the central substance of criminal law and disagreement with legal constructions regarding the mental element. Additionally, subcultural ambivalence is manifested in a distinction between the legal system and its agents—the one receiving general approval, the other disapproval. The subculture of delinquency shows antagonism to the law, but this antagonism is primarily directed to the officials who man the system. Antagonism takes the form of a jaundiced view of officials, a view which holds that their primary function

101

is not the administration of justice, but the perpetration of injustice.

The moral bind of law is loosened whenever a sense of injustice prevails. Law, whatever its guiding principle, trial by ordeal or due process, binds members of society to the extent that it maintains a semblance of even-handed administration. Guiding principles may vary but, whatever their substance, persistent violation of their spirit occurs at the peril of alienating the subjects of law and order. A legal system based on trial by ordeal is tenable, but one in which the internal logic of that system is regularly violated would to that extent lose the loyalty of its subjects. The legitimacy granted to law would be withdrawn.

Legal order is not simply a system of coercion.[1] The maintenance of law depends partly on its legitimacy. Among the basic elements of legitimate order is the belief on the part of subjects that some semblance of justice prevails. The common sense of Western traditions was well formulated in Augustine's rhetorical question, "What are states without justice but robber bands enlarged?" The cry of injustice is among the most fateful utterances of which man is capable—and no less consequential when expressed by schoolboys. It is tantamount to asserting that chaos or tyranny reign instead of order and society.

The sensing of injustice is a normal occurrence in any setting. However, its perception is heightened in the subculture of delinquency. The subculture aggravates and accentuates the sense of injustice among its adherents.[2]

A subculture does not consist merely of precepts that guide contemporary action. A subculture is rooted in the past. Consequently, subcultures accumulate events and incidents that are a part of the legacy transmitted to new cohorts. These events and incidents are the special histories of distinct subcultures. The subculture of delinquency possesses a rich folklore in which tales of injustice hold a prominent place. Thus, the subcultural adherent is not fully dependent on personal experience. His knowledge of local history supplies him with an initial set of incidents on which he may subsequently build. The subculture of delinquency is, among other things, a memory file that collects injustices.[3]

Moreover, the delinquent's sense of injustice is heightened by his standards. His standards of justice are rigorous, though not peculiarly so. His statements often seem unduly legalistic, and we infer that he is simply indulging in self-service. Delinquents often protest: "They got me on a bum rap; well, yea, I did it, but they didn't prove it." Surely, he is self-serving, but simultaneously he exhibits consensus with the legal view of crime. His definition of a crime departs somewhat from that of most criminologists and for that reason his statement is often taken to be a kind of smart-aleck evasion. "No, I never committed a crime like that—I mean to say I never got caught doing that." But his departure from the sociological definition of crime is precisely the same as that manifested in law. In that sense, his conception of crime is completely legalistic.

The commission of an illegal act by a responsible actor is not in itself a crime or delinquency. There is yet another necessary element before the designations criminal or delinquent are warranted. It is necessary from both the legal and the delinquent viewpoints. The additional element is *procedural*.

The legal basis for ascribing the terms crime or criminal differs considerably from sociological convention. Paul Tappan summarizes the juristic view:

Only those are criminals who have been adjudicated as such by the courts. Crime is an intentional act in violation of the criminal law . . . committed without defense or excuse, and penalized by the state as a felony or misdemeanor.[4]

The criminological or sociological conception is differentiated from that of law by Sutherland and Cressey:

In the democratic legal tradition even one who admits to having committed a crime is not designated a criminal until his criminality has been *proven* by means of the accepted court procedures. . . . However, for scientific purposes, it is not necessary that every decision be made in court; the criminologist must only know that a certain class of acts is defined as crime and that a particular person has committed an act of this class.[5]

The subcultural delinquent reveals his understandable preference for the legal view by an insistence on the necessity of a procedural element before the ascription of delinquency. The law stipulates, and the subculture of delinquency more than concurs, that a complicated and arduous administrative process precede the designation of persons as criminal or delinquent. Most commonly this process is called *justice*.

Justice and Its Components

What is justice? Surely, one must tread cautiously in matters that have perplexed so many. Just as surely, one should not expect universal agreement on the full meaning of justice. However, exploration of the minimal meaning of justice may be attempted and at any rate cannot be avoided. Injustice is the underlying condition of drift. It is a pervasive sense of delinquents and a preface to the assertion of irresponsibility—the immediate condition of drift. One can hardly inquire into the sensing of injustice without first considering the meaning of justice.

Great stress has traditionally been placed on the difficulties of defining justice. This is somewhat strange, since definitions of even more elusive entities—like society—are regularly hazarded by sociologists. Primarily, the pitfalls and the ensuing trepidations have resulted from a reluctance to settle for a minimal statement of the elements of justice and a related tendency to equate justice with moral order. The recognition that justice is "not coextensive with morality in general" [6] is an important step in the development of a minimal conception of justice.

A man guilty of gross cruelty to his child would often be judged to have done something morally *wrong, bad,* or even *wicked* or to have disregarded his moral *obligation* or duty to his child. But it would be strange to criticize his conduct as unjust. This is not because the word "unjust" is too weak in condemnatory force, but because the point of moral criticism in terms of justice or injustice is usually different from, and more specific than, the other types of general moral criticism which are appropriate in this particular case and are expressed by words like "wrong," "bad," or "wicked." "Unjust" would be appropriate if the man had arbitrarily selected one of his children for severer punishment than those given to others guilty of the same fault, or if he had punished the child for some offense without taking steps to see that he really was the wrongdoer.[7]

Thus, the terms just or unjust are often inappropriate. Defining justice is primarily a task of deciding when its use is appropriate and warranted. In reaching a decision of this sort we may capitalize on an asset that frequently remains unexploited.

The major dimensions of justice are known to most members of society in a crude and intuitive way because justice is a crucial aspect of the common sense of modern democratic nations.

Everyone has had the experience of feeling unjustly treated, of wondering whether he has acted fairly in some situation, of feeling that someone else was unjustly treated. People look at events in the community, the nation and the world and are aware that injustice is occurring. The experience and awareness of injustice are probably universal.[8]

Surely, there is variation in the conceptions of justice possessed by members of any society. However, variation or dissent is most likely to occur with respect to the precise point on a dimension that separates justice from injustice. The dimensions, themselves —the components or categories of justice—are more likely to achieve widespread agreement. Thus, we shall note that the subcultural delinquent conceives of the same categories of justice as conventional members of society. However, his subcultural perspective frequently prompts him to discern injustice where others may not. The precise point at which justice ends and injustice begins cannot be definitively stated. It is in some measure a matter of perspective and opinion, and thus eternally problematic. The subculture of delinquency utilizes this ambiguity in challenging the justice of legal administration.

The task of specifying the components of justice is expedited by one last operation—the use of a synonym. Whatever else justice may imply, it refers to fairness. Especially for children, but also for adults, much of the shared meaning of justice is captured by reference to fairness.

The distinctive features of justice and their special connexion with law begin to emerge if it is observed that most of the criticisms made in terms of just and unjust could almost equally well be conveyed by the words "fair" and "unfair." [9]

Conceiving of fairness as a synonym for justice helps in the search for a minimal definition since it substitutes a mundane term for one that is more esoteric and more loaded with conflicting and thus confusing precedent. Use of mundane terms allows us to conjure the sorts of experience commonly associated with the sensing of fairness or unfairness. "Fairness appears to be the short-hand method of describing the feeling tone involved in the sense of justice." [10]

The major meanings of fairness are captured, I believe, in the following assertions: it is only fair that some steps be taken to ascertain whether I was really the wrongdoer (cognizance); it is only fair that I be treated according to the same principles as others of my status (consistency); it is only fair that you who pass judgment on me sustain the right to do so (competence); it is only fair that some relationship obtain between the magnitude of what I have done and what you propose to do to me (commensurability); it is only fair that differences between the treatment of my status and others be reasonable and tenable (comparison). Each of these statements poses an elementary component of justice.[11]

Thus, the categories of justice raise as fundamental issues the questions of *cognizance, consistency, competence, commensurability,* and *comparison.* Cognizance, consistency, and competence will be discussed in the remainder of this chapter. Commensurability and comparison will be taken up in Chapter 5. Each of the issues and questions connected to them occurs to the subcultural delinquent and to most other members of modern society. In each case the perspective of subcultural delinquency and the structure of modern, enlightened juvenile justice combine to produce the appearance of rampant injustice.

Cognizance

It is fortunate that eternal judgment is rendered by an omniscient entity. The task requires such presence. The judgments rendered by human authority are somewhat less final and demand correspondingly less presence. However, some measure of cognizance is required if judgments are to gain legitimacy. The most elementary notion of fairness requires a mechanism that can associate or dissociate an actor with categories of good deeds and misdeeds. Generosity may be considered good and theft bad, but before praise or blame can be dispensed—before judgment can be rendered—some method must be devised by which a person may be classified as someone who is generous or a thief. The joining of personal action to differently evaluated categories is accomplished through evidence. Evidence may vary widely in form —from trial by ordeal to scientific experiment—but it remains constant in function. Evidence is symbolic of authoritative cognizance and serves to properly associate or dissociate actors and acts.

The association of actors with categories of offense is often a difficult task. Even when direct surveillance occurs and the culprit is caught red-handed, the association may not be simple. Since offense requires a mental element, being caught red-handed is not quite enough; the accused must be caught red-minded. Given the subcultural delinquent standards of justice and its conception of intent, even cases of this sort may present some difficulty. When there is no direct surveillance, and usually there is not, the development of evidence is obviously more difficult.

In the great majority of cases, the issue of cognizance seems hardly to arise—or so argue the proponents of contemporary juvenile justice. Juveniles usually confess their guilt. It is quite true that juveniles as well as adults usually confess their guilt, but this is of little consequence. The sense of injustice based on defective cognizance may be maintained despite the frequency of confession.

Confessions are not typically statements made by persons who willingly and joyfully present themselves to the nearest police officer. Confession is ordinarily preceded by suspcion, apprehension, and interrogation. An enforcement official's suspicion, apprehension, and interrogation of a guilty juvenile is usually enough to elicit a confession. However, the unfairness necessarily implicit in an efficient enforcement system that capitalizes on experience and hunch is not likely to be missed by the subcultural delinquent. Efficient enforcement systems contain agents who suspect, contact, apprehend, and interrogate only a few possible candidates. Most of us—the happy many—are rarely if ever contacted or questioned. "Why," the delinquent frequently asks, "are they always bugging *me?* Why is it that every time something happens, they pick on me?" The subcultural delinquent is not likely to appreciate the obvious answer, and for very good reason. There are no doubt sound and adequate reasons for never asking us, the conventional folk, if we committed a burglary, and continuously asking someone who is known as a delinquent. But despite the sound and obvious reasons for this selective procedure, the conventional folk would be remarkably obtuse to expect the subcultural delinquent to see and acknowledge the justice of such procedures. It seems to the subcultural delinquent remarkably unfair to exercise considerable cognizance over his activities and precious little over ours. Thus, even in those cases in which guilt is confessed, the subcultural delinquent may sense injustice because of selective procedures inherent in any efficient system of enforcement.[12] He feels that cognizance is unevenly exercised.

In a relatively small proportion of cases, delinquents protest their innocence. These cases are eligible to become part of the subcultural folklore. Since a subculture selectively collects events and incidents, it is not necessary that extraordinary violations of justice—atrocity tales—be claimed in anything approaching a majority of contacts with legal agents. The sense of injustice is conveyed through the collective and selective experiences encountered by contemporary delinquents and their local predecessors. Thus, a sense of injustice may be pervasive despite the statistical infrequency of actually contesting a charge.

Moreover, the legalistic standards espoused in the subculture mean that the accused may protest his innocence despite the fact that he committed the act. Subcultural delinquents frequently complain of "bum raps." Typically, the observer reacts to the claim with either sympathetic gullibility or urbane skepticism. Both responses are inadequate in that neither inquires into the meaning of the phrase. Thus, both reactions miss what is conveyed. This is a "bum rap":

The sovereign lords . . . were raiding us almost daily. . . . I was planning to cruise through their turf . . . blasting the Lords with our . . . guns. . . . "I got my eye on a good tank for it," JoJo said. "A beat Chevy convertible. It must be a hot car; it's been parked in one spot for a week. Nobody'll miss it." [13]

When the boys had started the car and were about to drive away in it, a prowl car drew up in front of them. They were caught by the police. Our exemplary delinquent states:

That is how I was busted for the last time—on a bum rap. Thirteen was my unlucky number. "Honest to God, Mr. Ahearn," I swore, "I didn't steal that car. I was just sitting in it. I don't know who stole it. I didn't even know it was stolen. That's the truth, Mr. Ahearn." [14]

Apparently, no one during this incident explained that his notion of "bum rap" was rather peculiar. In point of fact, if we may believe the delinquent's report, his perception was confirmed. Officer Ahearn allegedly replied:

I believe you Frenchy. But if I can't get you for something you did, I'll settle for something you didn't do.[15]

A "bum rap" may refer to being busted for an offense that one did not commit *or* to an inadequate demonstration or proof of an association between an offense and the accused.

The mechanism by which act and actor are associated—evidence—is in some juvenile cases not visibly put in operation. Most juvenile courts do not possess an adequate mechanism for associating the actor with the infraction. It is mistakenly believed that this presents no problem because more than 90 per cent of juveniles confess their guilt. But this reckons without the capacity of subcultures to select exceptional cases and to figuratively collect a dossier on the occasional omissions of police and court. Furthermore, it reckons without the delinquent's knowledge and unkind assessment of the selective procedures which ordinarily underlie apprehension and interrogation. Thus, proof may be a ritual, as some spokesmen of enlightened jurisprudence have suggested, but it is a ritual of enormous consequence. Each time it is omitted, the incident may enter the unwritten annals of subcultural delinquency.

The dependence on confession as the typical form of evidence may be productive of an additional perception of injustice. Occasionally, a member of a delinquent band will "take the rap" for one of his associates. This may be done voluntarily or through coercion. The strategy underlying such antics is ordinarily sound but occasionally it backfires. Subcultural delinquents come to realize that prior to actual incarceration they are normally granted a generous quota of chances consisting of police reprimands, citations, informal probations, formal probations, referrals to the Youth Authority with a stay of sentence, and a variety of other sanctions. Thus, a proxy may appear in order to forestall the ultimate sanction—incarceration—of a fellow member who has used up his chances. Normally, the proxy is put on probation, as predicted, but occasionally, if the offense is serious or if there is a crackdown, the strategy may backfire and the proxy may be incarcerated. In either case, the proxy may sense injustice, despite his complicity in the fraud. If he is put on probation, as predicted, he may retrospectively sense injustice in later years when his record as it is read to him seems a bit longer than it ought to be. If the strategy backfires and he is imprisoned, he may sense the injustice immediately. Enforcement officials have failed to exercise cognizance. Because of their reliance on confession, they have allowed the subculture to which the proxy adheres to capitalize on the camaraderie it expects, or to rely on the exploitation of members it sometimes uses when such camaraderie cannot be encouraged. Enforcement officials, because they have failed to exercise strict cognizance and instead relied on confessions, become implicated in the fraudulent conspiracy initiated by their delinquent charges.

Consistency

Consistency is the expectation that treatment according to the same principle extends over a category of persons. It is perhaps the fundamental element of justice. In its simplest form, justice in law:

consists in no more than taking seriously the notion that what is to be applied to a multiplicity of different persons is the same general rule, undeflected by prejudice, interest or caprice. This impartiality is what the procedural standards known . . . as principles of "Natural Justice" are designed to secure. Hence, though the most odious laws may be justly applied, we have in the bare notion of applying a general rule of law, the germ at least of justice. [16]

Consistency is the element that insures the comparative nature of justice. Consistency, or its absence, may be sensed only over a series of cases. Thus, the expectation of consistency directs the attention of the accused to the question of how *others* are treated. Justice taken as consistency cannot be assessed or vouched for without prompting an incessant and sometimes irritating concern with decisions that are not one's personal matters. A concern with consistency necessarily converts us into busybodies.

Inconsistency is not the same as inequality. Inconsistency is unreasonable or arbitrary inequality. Fifteen year olds do not receive the same treatment as those who are four and they do not expect it. Thus, consistency does not preclude reasonable or tenable inequality—that is, inequality based on acceptable distinctions.

The point is that the inequalities resulting from the law must make sense. If decisions differ, some discernible distinction must be found bearing an intelligible relation to the difference in result. The sense of injustice revolts against whatever is unequal by caprice. The arbitrary, although indispensable to many of the law's daily operations, is always suspect; it becomes unjust when it discriminates between indistinguishables.[17]

The subculture of delinquency collects examples of inconsistency. Inconsistencies are bound to occur at least occasionally in any administration of justice since agents may use slightly differing standards. However, the impression of inconsistency, if not the substance, is likely to increase enormously when two related conditions appear. The sense of inconsistency is likely to be heightened when legal agents possess great discretion or when the principles that guide decision are diffusely or mysteriously delineated. Both of these conditions appear in the juvenile court, a court that has ultimate jurisdiction over the legal treatment of juveniles who are accused of offense, and ultimate authority over all of the agents and agencies dealing with them.

The Impression of Inconsistency and Individualized Justice [18]

Individualized justice is *the* basic precept in the philosophy of the juvenile court.[19] More generally, it is commended to all officials who deal with juveniles. We should, it is suggested by enlightened professionals, gear our official dispositions to suit the individual needs of the accused rather than respond in automatic fashion to the offense that he has allegedly committed. The relating of disposition to individual needs instead of to the offense is a central aspect of the modern *treatment* viewpoint. I wish to suggest that a principle of individualized justice creates a setting which is conducive to the sensing of rampant inconsistency. It is that milieu in which the sense of injustice flourishes. Thus, it may be taken as a prime instance of conventional subterranean support of subcultural delinquent beliefs.

Equality, equity, and individualized justice are concepts whose use—or misuse—has led to considerable confusion. The confusion emanating from the misuse of concepts has been of social consequence in that part of the injustice sensed by delinquents is a response to what to them must appear a specious variety of word magic. The sense of injustice develops around the crucial differences of meaning between equity and individualized justice; it especially develops when authoritative officials display a studied indifference to the important differences between each of the concepts.

Equity in criminal proceedings is best viewed as a *doctrine*— a qualification or legitimate exception to the *principle* of equality. The principle is that we treat people equally, which is to say that we consistently apply the same limited set of criteria in the disposition of cases. Occasionally, the justice yielded by the application of these criteria strikes us as patently unjust. It takes no account of events *which in that particular case* appear in sufficiently great measure as to overwhelm the relevance of ordinary criteria. Equity justice in criminal proceedings is almost by definition extraordinary justice. We allow the qualification of a principle of equality through the occasional consideration of special mitigating circumstances partially to maintain the sense that we dispense justice, but mainly to forestall the always imminent danger of continuous mounting of additional criteria. It is the avoidance of this latter possibility that is the major function of the doctrine of equity.

Let us say that in a particular situation of judgment the principle guiding disposition includes the consideration of offense and prior record but precludes the consideration of economic or family status. Moreover, let us assume in this particular case, because of the extreme circumstances of poverty experienced by the defendant, the extreme parental abuse to which he had been subjected, and the uncontestably close correspondence between the nature of his offense and these circumstances, that no reasonable judge could in good conscience maintain their irrelevance. The function of the doctrinal qualification of equity is to maintain *in principle* that such considerations are irrelevant, but to allow their relevance in *this particular* case. Is this simply casuistry? No, it is not. We may only wish to consider events like economic or family status in *extraordinary instances,* in which case the formulation of a principle is extremely difficult and unwise. Moreover, we may wish to *limit* the number of criteria included in the principle to those that for the time being we regard as eternally relevant. Otherwise, the addition of legitimate criteria to be used in disposition may be continuous, resulting in a situation in which the criteria are too numerous to provide clear and publicly comprehensible guides to action.

Individualized justice differs fundamentally from equity. Equity in criminal proceedings is a doctrinal qualification of the principle of equality. Individualized justice is *itself* a principle. It is a principle which on first appearances seems merely to substitute one set of relevant criteria for another. This it does—and considerably more. It does more than simply substitute frames of relevance for two reasons. To understand why this is so, we must first appreciate that the usual claim that equality is violated by individualized justice is at least in theory wrong, or beside the point.

The principle of equality is a misnomer. All principles, to the extent that they are formulated, stress equality in that they commend a *framework of relevance* by which all cases are to be judged. The principle of equality can be reduced to the dictum of treating like cases in like manner. This, as Hart suggests, is an empty formula unless we are told the criteria by which to determine the like cases. The principle of equality refers to a specific set of substantive criteria that are awarded central relevance and, historically, to a set of considerations that were specifically and momentously precluded. Its meaning, especially in criminal proceedings, has been to give a central and unrivaled position in the framework of relevance to considerations of *offense* and conditions closely related to offense like prior record, and to more or less preclude considerations of status and circumstance. This has been the overall substantive meaning of the principle of equality and the only grounds on which it may be distinguished from other principles, which logically are equally equal. Thus, strictly speaking, the principle of equality should be called the *principle of offense*.

The principle of individualized justice is a distinct departure from that of offense, but not in the sense of liquidating the norm of equality. Principles cannot depart from the norm of equality. Their function is to suggest a framework of relevance by which we may infer the meaning of the recommendation that we treat like cases alike. Internal equality of treatment within a category is the very meaning of a principle. A principle informs us of the particular mode of equality we will apply to juveniles even though juveniles as a category may be treated differently than adults. Such different treatment may be justified on the grounds that juvenile and adult matters are not like cases. The separate jurisdiction of juvenile and adult matters, the differences in the statutory expectations, and the differences in procedure may be tenable or untenable. But in either case that issue should not be confused with the internal equality of treatment suggested by a principle.[20]

If the principle of individualized justice does not differ from that of offense with respect to equality, how does it differ? It differs in two fundamental ways. First, it is much more inclusive: it contains many more items in its framework of relevance. Second, the kinds of criteria it includes are more diffuse than those commended in the principle of offense.

The principle of individualized justice is more inclusive than the principle of offense. It contains many more criteria in its framework of relevance. Its greater inclusiveness is assured by the fact that the older principle, that of offense, is included in the newer one, that of individualized justice. Spokesmen for individualized justice do not suggest that offense is irrelevant; rather, that it is one of many considerations that are to be used in arriving at a sound disposition.[21] Offense, like many other forms of behavior, is to be taken as an indication or "symptom" of the juvenile's personal and social disorder. The principle of individualized justice suggests that disposition is to be guided by a *full understanding* of the client's personal and social character and by his "individual needs." This view is well captured by the slogan which suggests that nowadays the treatment fits the individual whereas in olden times the punishment fit the crime. Needless to say, the transition from olden to modern times is taken as one manifestation of a major historical transformation commonly called the enlightenment. I want to suggest that the character of this transformation is completely missed and distorted if we take it as part of the wider process of enlightenment. We come closer to assessing its real character by insisting that its impact has been the very opposite of enlightenment. The consequence of the principle of individualized justice has been mystification.

The principle of individualized treatment is a mystification. Indeed, it is one of the very best examples of mystification in current society. To the extent that it prevails, its function is to obscure the process of decision and disposition rather than to enlighten it. The principle of individualized justice results in a frame of relevance that is so large, so all-inclusive, that any relation between the criteria of judgment and the disposition remains obscure.

Every practicing sociologist knows that the lay version of *gestalt*—the idea that everything matters—has come to obscure rather than to enlighten social process. The principle of individualized justice, and the lay version of *gestalt* that ultimately underlies it, is no less a mystification in the process of judgment. The inclusion of personal and social character as relevant criteria in judgment has been consequential. Its consequence has been that hardly anyone, and least of all the recipients of judgment who have some special interest in these matters, is at all sure what combinations of the widely inclusive relevant criteria yield what sorts of specific disposition. Indeed, no one has even attempted such a task. The task is manifestly an immense if not an impossible one.

A combination of impoverished economic position, a marginal scholastic record, a particular kind of disrupted family situation, a current infraction of burglary, and two past citations for auto theft yields a disposition. What disposition? If we ask court agents, they will honestly and appropriately answer that it depends. On what does it depend? It depends on other factors. On what other factors? Well, perhaps on a diagnosis of the child's personality, but that too depends. On what does that depend? Ultimately, it depends on the needs of the child. And, on what do these needs depend? And eventually we come to the final and only possible answer. It depends on the professional training, experience, and judgment of the court agents. Any system with an extremely wide frame of relevance in which the items included in the frame are neither specifically enumerated nor weighted must come to rely heavily on professional judgment.

This great reliance on professional judgment is the key to the mystery contained in the juvenile court, and more generally the riddle of the whole administration of juvenile justice. The whole system depends enormously on the judicious use of judgment. Does not every system? To some limited extent, yes, but only to the extent that frames of relevance are inclusive rather than limited. What I have described is a system of rampant discretion. The reliance on judgment based on experience and training or, to use an older term, wisdom, is the distinctive feature of any system promoting individualized justice as a *principle* rather than viewing equity as a *doctrinal qualification* of some other narrower principle.

What of the clarity of the many criteria that are included in a principle of individualized justice? Surely, the principle of offense is itself no pinnacle of clarity. As I suggested earlier, offenses may be diffusely defined and the joining of actors to categories is usually problematic, at least in some measure. However, this concession of obvious legal shortcomings should not obscure the equally obvious point that compared to most systems the law works arduously and sometimes even successfully toward clarity and specificity of definitions of offense. Little that is included in the frame of relevance sponsored by those guided by a principle of individualized justice approaches even the most vaguely formulated criminal statute. Indeed, many spokesmen for individualized justice would not want it so. If the categories of offense vary by jurisdiction, and if the same terms often pertain to different referents, what can be said of the categories implicit in the more inclusive framework stressing personal and social background? Many of the categories implicit in those frameworks at best approach the clarity of the most diffuse legal categories, say, incorrigibility.

Some categories used by court agents have rather specific referents, for instance, age, occupation of father, and perhaps school performance. Others, which occupy an important place in the frame of relevance, are hardly as specific as the legal term incorrigibility. The "home situation," which is regularly described in the probation worker's report, is an example. What is a home situation? With what degree of assurance may we utter the designations adequate, inadequate, or poor? And what forms of evidence are used to associate or dissociate persons with each of these categories? Finally, there are the categories of personality and the multitude of assessments that appear in each of them. My aim here is not to criticize the social and psychological categories that are used and sometimes abused by court agents. In some instances, they happen to be the best we can do and in many kinds of research they do well enough. The point is that compared to offense categories they are necessarily more diffuse. They are more diffuse not so much because lawyers are more practiced in the arts of clarity than those who create social and personal categories, though they surely are, but because the degree of complexity in the respective tasks fundamentally differs. It is, at this juncture and perhaps eternally, more difficult to locate and specifically define relevant personal and social categories than offense categories. Consequently, the criteria implicit in a principle of individualized justice are not only more numerous than those implicit in a principle of offense; they are more diffusely defined, too. Thus, court agents are dependent on wisdom in a double sense. They must use wisdom in deciding which portion of the wide frame of relevance they will assign greatest weight and thus invoke in any particular case. Moreover, they must use their judgment in applying whichever portion of the frame of relevance they choose since each portion in itself tends to be diffusely defined.

The reliance on judgment which in turn depends on the wisdom acquired through professional training and experience marks the juvenile court. Realization that the reliance on judgment and wisdom is an essential and distinctive feature of the court allows us to characterize the variety of justice that is dispensed within it. Such designation is important even if as an approximation since the juvenile's reaction to court and especially the potential for sensing injustice depends on the *kind* of court that regularly services him. Despite the considerable variation among juvenile courts,

I suggest that they by and large approximate a single type. The variations are around a single theme. Indeed, one can and should paradoxically suggest that great variation in the practice and sentiment of the dispensing units is and always has been a central characteristic of this kind of justice. The claim that there is great variation from one juvenile court to another within the same jurisdiction, or even the same building, has traditionally been taken as a warning against generalization concerning the court. I suggest contrarily that the great variation from court to court is one of the most important and revealing generalizations one can make about the type of justice regularly dispensed in juvenile courts.

The juvenile court is not the first court marked by great variation among the dispensing units. That sort of variation is a general feature of *kadi* justice—the brand of justice most closely approximated by the juvenile court, to the extent that it is guided by the canons of individualized justice.[22] Kadi is a variety of justice that is unified by the great variation of practice and sentiment appearing within its realm. The particular form taken depends mainly on the special attributes of judgment and wisdom possessed by the kadi. Max Rheinstein describes the kadi as:

The Moslem judge who sits in the market place, and, at least seemingly, renders his decisions without any reference to rules or norms but in what appears to be a completely free evaluation of the particular merits of every single case. The type (substantive irrationality) would also be approximated by that kind of wise man who, ably applying the Solomonic hunch, would seem to represent the ideal of the German School of free law or the American Realists.[23]

Rheinstein's description of the kadi is enlightening for two related reasons. First, it implicitly alerts us to what is obvious but nonetheless warrants reminder. The kadi does not really render his decisions without any reference to rules or norms. What the kadi in all likelihood does should by now be obvious. He operates with an extremely wide frame of relevance in which, in principle, everything matters. In each particular case he implicitly chooses that section of the frame of relevance he wishes to invoke. He is under no sustained obligation to choose the same section of the frame of relevance in every case. That is the kadi's distinctive prerogative which he may or may not exercise. The second matter enlightened by Rheinstein's description is implicit in the same remark. The kadi *seems* to render decisions without reference to rules or norms and is engaged in what *appears to be* a completely free evaluation of the particular merits of each case. Rheinstein does not say to whom matters seem that way though I suppose he means untutored students of law. That may be true but it is of no immediate relevance. Of immediate relevance is the sense in which the kadi seems *to the recipients of justice* to render decisions without reference to rules or norms. *It appears to them* that he is engaged in a completely free evaluation of the case.

Before turning to the way in which kadi justice appears to its recipients, let us explore its meaning a little further. Max Weber distinguishes among rational, empirical, kadi, and charismatic justice. He says:

> The rational interpretation of law on the basis of strictly formal conceptions stands opposite the kind of adjudication that is primarily bound to sacred traditions. The single case that cannot be unambiguously decided by tradition is either settled by concrete "revelation" (oracle, prophetic dicta, or ordeal—that is by charismatic justice) or —and only these cases interest us here—*by informal judgments rendered in terms of concrete ethical or other practical evaluations.* This is *"kadi justice,"* as R. Schmidt fittingly called it. Or formal judgments are rendered, though not by subsumption under rational concepts, but by drawing on "analogies" and by depending upon and interpreting concrete "precedents." This is "empirical justice." [24]

Thus, kadi stands between empirical and charismatic justice. All three, kadi, empirical, and charismatic justice, depart from rational justice which is based on "strictly formal conceptions." But the three differ with respect to the kinds of tradition that guide judgments: empirical justice is guided by the interpretation of concrete *legal precedents;* kadi justice, by concrete *ethical and practical valuations;* charismatic justice, by concrete *revelation.*

Thus far, I have suggested the similarity between the contemporary juvenile court and kadi justice. But if the juvenile court is an instance of kadi justice, it is a very special instance. Weber correctly considers ideal kadi justice a nonbureaucratic form of domination. So nonbureaucratic is the ideal instance of kadi that

Weber perceptively saw in it a strain toward the charismatic form. He says:

Kadi-justice knows no reasoned judgment whatever. Nor does empirical justice of the pure type give any reasons which in our sense could be called rational. The concrete valuational character of Kadi-justice can advance to a prophetic break with all tradition. . . . All non-bureaucratic forms of domination display a peculiar co-existence: *on the one hand, there is a sphere of strict traditionalism, and on the other, a sphere of free arbitrariness and lordly grace.* . . .[25]

Surely, juvenile justice shows little sign of advancing "to a prophetic break with all tradition." Contemporary juvenile justice is a peculiar form of kadi justice in which the reliance on judgment and wisdom persists but is fundamentally modified and distorted by the strange, one might almost say unseemly, setting in which it appears. The juvenile court exercises kadi justice in a bureaucratic context. This is a feature of the juvenile court to which I shall return in the discussion of the ways in which the *competence* of some of its agents is challenged by its juvenile clientele. Now I want simply to note the peculiarity inherent in the transfer of an independent kadi from his original and natural setting, the market place, to a career position in the wider bureaucratic establishment entrusted with the administration of justice. The current setting of kadi is, to say the least, a very different kind of market place.

What is so peculiar about kadi justice being dispensed within a bureaucratic context? Kadi justice, both in general and in its current rendition stressing the principle of individualized treatment, tends in the main to widen discretion, whereas bureaucratization tends in the main to limit discretion.[26]

Legal bureaucracies, like any other, must concern themselves with routines, work flow, public relations, maintenance of reasonable internal harmony, record keeping, and a variety of other forms of business. What does this tell us about the way in which the setting will influence the principle of justice being espoused? It informs us, I believe, that the kadi will undergo persistent and often self-imposed stress, especially since he happens to be the manager of the court as well as its kadi, to bend his decisions in a manner that will serve institutional needs. The wide discretion given him by the principle of individualized judgment is limited in a way that will be consistent with the bureaucratic norms of efficiency, good public relations, and the maintenance of harmony and *esprit de corps* among his underlings. Thus, the kadi's initially free-wheeling choice is restricted by his structural situation.

However, it would be inaccurate as well as unfair to leave the discussion at that. The kadi in the juvenile court is susceptible to another set of pressures because of the peculiar sort of bureaucracy in which he finds himself, and specifically because of the strange sentiments espoused by many of his underlings. In some measure, and the measure is closely related to the extent to which the court is guided by the principle of individualized justice, the judge precariously rules over what to him must surely seem a *social-work* bureaucracy. If internal harmony is to be maintained, if work is to flow, if the embarrassment of frequent reversal of the probation worker's recommendation is to be avoided, and all of these are in some measure necessary, then the kadi must succumb to another set of pressures. These too serve to limit his discretion. In what direction do the social work pressures push him? There are two ways of answering that question. One would be to indulge in and describe the mystifications that pervade social-work theory. This would be of little help since they merely duplicate and are in fact the basis of the kadi's aimless guide to action—the principle of individualized justice. The second way of answering the question is more open to controversy, but I believe it to be true in the main. The pressure exerted on the judge by his social-work underlings is, to state it simply, for *mercy*.

Now, a statement as bald as that, especially when it seems to confirm the public criticism of the social-work view, surely seems calculated to provoke disagreement from the practitioners in that profession. Many spokesmen for social work would argue that I have misunderstood their basic point of view, taken it out of context and thus distorted it. That claim would be partly true. I have taken the quality of mercy out of the context in which it appears in social-work pronouncements, and in that sense distorted their complex and sometimes mysterious message. My only defense is that I believe that the kadi oversimplifies the message of his social-work underlings in a manner similar to that expressed here. It seems to him that what his underlings ask for most of the time is mercy for the offender. He may understand, appreciate, and even concur with the elaborate social-work theory that underlies the plea for one sort of mercy or another. However, that is of little consequence. By this time, the kadi is seeking a guide to action, and the flimsiest sort of justification may suffice.

The kadi is subject to one final pressure. Since he manages the court, it is he who is ultimately responsible to the public. He will have to explain to those specialists in indignation—newspaper-men—why the 17-year-old murderer of an innocent matron was allowed to roam the streets, on probation, when just last year he was booked for mugging. This is no easy question to answer. Somehow, an invoking of the principle of individualized justice and a justification of mercy on the basis of accredited social-work theory hardly seems appropriate on these occasions. Thus, the kadi anticipates the situation. He worries about it. He talks about it to almost anyone who cares to listen. It is the awesome hazard of his calling. Consequently, he becomes subjected to a pressure exactly contradicting that emanating from his underlings. It is his sense that the public demands *severity*. And, in a sense, he is quite right. The public, whenever it speaks to the kadi, does seem to be demanding severity.

In summary, the contemporary kadi's situation is one in which the principle of individualized justice gives him incredibly wide discretion and incredibly little guide for action. But his traditional freedom is restricted by the peculiar bureaucratic setting in which it appears. His judgment and wisdom may reign but only precariously since he is simultaneously the manager of the court and must thus concern himself with public relations, internal harmony, efficient work flow, and the rest. How does the kadi handle and respond to the pressures in which he is caught? The answer to that question returns us to what must seem to the reader a round-about way of arriving at the basis of the delinquent's sense of injustice. But there is no other way. The *delinquent's* sense of injustice is partially rooted in the *kadi's* response to his own delicate situation.

The kadi's responses to the crosspressures obviously vary but not as much as one might imagine. If we pay attention to what he actually does and not to the rhetoric by which he justifies his dispositions, some interesting and by no means unprecedented things seem to happen. A first order of business is to merely get through the day's work. The flow of juvenile cases is something to behold. Falling behind is consequential since there are other points on the juvenile assembly line, detention halls, for instance, that will suffer pile-ups. Cases must be handled routinely and efficiently or else there will be complaints to the management from other parts of the system. Much of the real work and real decision making is done behind the scenes where the recipient of justice cannot observe it. It is completely obscured from him. His court hearing is typically perfunctory, though occasionally a case is rather thoroughly explored.

Within the limits set by the demands of time, efficiency, and work flow, the kadi's wisdom and judgment may operate. He must decide which portion of the wide frame of relevance to invoke in each case, and in every case he is subjected to the remaining cross-pressures; one calling for severity, the other for mercy; one emanating from far-off and occasional critics, the other from nearby and ever-present underlings with whom he must work; one irrelevant to the day-to-day administration of an efficient court, the other crucially relevant; but one representing what he takes to be public opinion, the other what he takes to be professional opinion; and one holding the sanction of public scandal, the other of professional criticism. Indeed, the kadi must be bestowed with judgment and wisdom. His frame of relevance for the disposition of cases is truly one in which many things matter.

His typical solution, and in a sense it is the only solution open to ordinary mortals, is compromise. However, his compromise is of the sort that suggests the surrender of authority rather than a wily manipulation of sovereignty. He renders unto each camp what seems to be their due, and, if his social-work underlings display the normal sensitivity of those who ply that trade, they will protect their kadi from embarrassment by not asking him for what is not properly theirs. Moreover, as social-work colleagues begin to work the other side of the system, as they appear in what used to be called prisons, the kadi's underlings may no longer see incarceration as necessarily a violation of mercy. Under those conditions, the important thing is to place the juvenile in a good prison. The kadi, on his part, may come to see that probation, which is what he regularly utters in giving his underlings their due, is not without elements of severity.

Thus, the system comes to attain a certain precarious equilibrium. The only problem, and it is one that constantly threatens the arrangement, is to decide which clients are to be helped by being rendered unto probation, thus satisfying the professional underlings, and which to be helped by rendering them unto prison, thus satisfying the public specialists in indignation. Once on probation or in prison, the juvenile can begin getting his individualized treatment.

But how decide which recipients of justice to render unto whom? The answer, I think, is a fascinating instance of the duplicity of social arrangements. It is a duplicity that is faintly observable to some of the canny juveniles who pass through the court. It is missed by almost everyone who works the system or passes through it. Some delinquents, probably a small minority, sense what is happening and on that sense they base their jaundiced assessment of the whole system. The others, probably a large majority, never themselves sense the duplicity and thus continue to be mystified by the proceedings before them. Even if they are given the key to the mystery by others, they have never themselves unlocked it, and so in some measure the feeling of being mystified persists. The mystery, of course, is how a court that publicly announces adherence to an aimless guide to action—the principle of individualized justice—makes decisions and quickly disposes of cases. Its adherence to this principle is not merely textbook material; it is regularly flaunted in court before its bewildered clients.

How does the court make decisions and thus solve the problem of whom to render unto whom? I believe the answer to be quite simple. The court's solution contains two elements. One, the main part of the solution, is to more or less reinstore—*sub rosa*—the *principle of offense*. Those delinquents who sense this flagrant violation of the court's publicly espoused philosophy take the amazing hullaballoo regarding individualized justice and treatment to be pious cant, abortive mystification, and patent "snow job." Are they right in their assessment? Not completely, because the concern with individual characteristics and with treatment is not completely surrendered by the court. These concerns remain but they are transformed, *as they must be* in any ongoing system of bureaucratic domination, into workable doctrines that may routinely function as enlightening guides to action rather than mystifying obstacles. The workable bureaucratic equivalents of the stress on extraordinary individual characteristics—equity—and the philosophy of treatment are the doctrines of *parental sponsorship* and *residential availability.*

Let us briefly explore the workings of this emergent system. My suggestion is that the court, like any social institution that has to get work done, has revised and fundamentally modified—one might even say distorted—its historic endowment. This fundamental modification was necessary because the principle of individualized justice and treatment turned out, upon the investigation inherent in judicial experience, to be an aimless guide to action. The emergent system was a happy synthesis because it allowed the kadi to continue speaking in the terms accredited by enlightened court philosophy. Moreover, it helped him resolve and respond to the systematic crosspressures he encountered.

In the emergent synthesis, the principle of offense is reinstituted as the central principle guiding disposition. It is importantly qualified by doctrines that allude to, but routinize, the sentiments of individual justice and treatment. This means that whether a juvenile goes to some manner of prison or is put on some manner of probation—the alternative sentences from which the kadi mainly chooses—depends first, on a traditional rule-of-thumb assessment of the total risk of danger and thus scandal evident in the juvenile's current offense and prior record of offenses; this initial reckoning is then importantly qualified by an assessment of the potentialities of "out-patient supervision" and the guarantee against scandal inherent in the willingness and ability of parents or surrogates to sponsor the child. If the reckoning of danger and thus potential scandal is extremely high, then no amount of parental or surrogate sponsorship will result in mere probation. The offender will be rendered unto those who support and man the prison. If the reckoning of danger is moderate then the decision will turn on an assessment of the presence, the amount, the quality, and the dependability of parental sponsorship. The cumulative reckoning of offense and prior record being equal, those with adequate sponsorship will be rendered unto probation, and those inadequately sponsored to prison. If the reckoning of danger is very low, then only those with virtually no visible or foreseeable parental sponsorship whatever will go to prison. This may all seem reasonable to the reader and in a way it is. But do not expect it to seem either reasonable or just to a neglected or otherwise inadequately sponsored recipient of this sort of wisdom.

The second doctrinal qualification on the principle of offense pertains to the availability of residential treatment or, to revert to the older usage, prison space. The judge, like his academic counterparts in the humanistic or inexact disciplines, grades on a curve. The cutting point between D (probation) and F (prison) is not based simply on an intrinsic assessment made on the individual merits or demerits of the case. Relativity commonly intrudes, especially when we fall short of complete faith in our intrinsic evaluations. The judge may be able to sort juveniles into those who are better or worse, or, as he may put it, those who require more or less help, but it is difficult for him to know the precise or even reasonable dividing line between those who are to receive probation and those who will go to prison. Thus, the dividing line may vacillate somewhat depending on residential availability. The main reckoning based on the consideration of current and prior offense qualified by an assessment of the presence and dependability of parental sponsorship is sufficient to roughly order juvenile clients along a spectrum ranging from very good to very poor risks. But this reckoning does not tell where to draw the dividing line. Individual cases may be ordered along a curve, but there are no cutting points. Justice must possess cutting points in order to achieve decision. Thus, when the original principles guiding a legal institution are so aimless as to forget cutting points, those who man the institution will themselves elaborate them over the course of experience. The cutting point is supplied by the publicly obscure doctrine of residential availability.

Does this mean that whether or not a child goes to prison depends ultimately on whether or not there is bed space available? Not at all, though it often seems that way to the untutored juvenile delinquent and even to some who study him. Residential availability is a doctrine, not a principle. Like all doctrines, but especially unspoken ones, it may or may not be invoked. The judge is not committed to the curve as a principle. Like many professors he uses the curve as an aid, as a doctrinal qualification on a principle of intrinsic evaluations. The doctrine of residential availability is wittingly or unwittingly invoked only when *no obvious decision* ensues from the main reckoning based on the principle of offense and the primary doctrine of parental sponsorship. In many, perhaps most, cases, the decision is obvious. It seems to the judge that *anyone* faced with this case and exposed to the same crosspressures would decide in the same way. By and large, he is correct. There are many cases in which the juvenile obviously presents a great risk of danger and thus scandal. If there is no residential space for him, let it be made, thunders the kadi. After all, he is a man of some authority, and not merely a bureaucratic minion. Space will be found or made. On the other hand, there are many cases in which the juvenile obviously presents little risk of danger and thus scandal. If there is a great deal of space available, let it lie fallow, reasons the kadi. After all, he is no tyrant. Moreover, he has been regularly exposed to the view that prisons sometimes cause crime rather than prevent it. Thus, in many cases the doctrine of residential availability is hardly needed or used. But in some cases, probably a small minority, the decision is far from obvious. In those few cases, the choice between probation or prison is exceedingly difficult. In those cases, the judge is likely to invoke the doctrine of residential availability. What else is there? The judge and his helpers have already teased whatever guidance they could from the principle of offense and the doctrine of parental sponsorship. The judge like his academic counterpart must make a decision. And, like the professor, he takes refuge in the curve which serves him well. It supplies him with both a decision and in some measure a vocabulary by which to justify the decision, whatever the eventual outcome.

Let us suppose that the judge is faced with a particular case in which choice between probation and prison is exceedingly difficult. In such a case, he may reason that, since the residential facilities are already vastly overcrowded, no purpose would be served by sending yet another juvenile there. The offender would not be helped and the services to the juveniles already in prison would be reduced by the additional client. Thus, the judge is given guidance by the doctrine of residential availability. Moreover, in the unhappy event that the juvenile breaks the law in an especially flagrant or brutal way while on probation, thus precipitating a scandal, the judge may retrospectively invoke the reason for his ill-fated decision. He justifies his action on grounds that make sense even to the specialists in indignation. He has already been sure to make frequent public statements calling for more residential facilities. *Now,* the judge makes clear that *this* juvenile would have been incarcerated had there only been available space. In this situation, the judge plays the part of bureaucratic minion. Though he has some authority, he now stresses the limits on it. The journalistic specialists in indignation take his cue. There will be a scandal, but it will be directed to higher authorities—to the department of corrections who will in turn direct the specialists to the governor's office. But all of this, while interesting and perhaps even satisfying to the kadi, is strictly speaking no longer his business. Through the occasional court use of the doctrine of residential availability, and through frequent reference to it in other public contexts, the kadi is able to invoke it retrospectively, thus absolving himself of responsibility for scandal.

The emergent reliance on the reinstituted principle of offense, qualified not by equity and treatment but by their routinized equivalents, parental sponsorship and residential availability, is founded on the connected facts that they can provide the kadi with substantive guides to action, allow him to maintain peace in the internal court establishment, and deflect or at least minimize the chances of public scandal introduced by the external presence of specialists in indignation. This amalgam emerged and persists because it was a workable accommodation to the originally aimless principles of individualized justice and treatment. In considerable measure this accommodating amalgam has satisfied everyone who partakes of the system—everyone, that is, who matters. The emergence of this amalgam has been overlooked, especially the reinstituting of the principle of offense, because it has all taken place hidden by the verbal mystifications characteristic of the court. Dispositions are rendered in the language of individualized justice and treatment. Moreover, the chances that internal mystification would survive and be perpetrated on the wider public were enhanced by the fortunate belief that outsiders should not ordinarily be allowed to observe—in the interests of the child— the happenings in court. Thus, the notion of confidentiality maintained the mystification in that journalists have almost never been allowed in juvenile court and were thus prevented from applying their special skill to the court itself. Only a few professionals, usually sociologists, sometimes lawyers, are occasionally given special dispensation to observe court hearings. These professionals, in the past twenty years, have been almost universally critical of what they have observed. But the mystification obtains because they are of little public consequence, and because they have limited their analyses to criticizing the operation of the court and recommending additional legal safeguards instead of analyzing it as an emergent system.

The present amalgam survives in the court because everyone who matters is satisfied with the arrangement. It is, as we say, functional. In a moment, I shall argue that it is not so very functional, as soon as we introduce the juvenile offender's perspective into the system. Until that boorish introduction, however, let us briefly ponder the equilibrium that has emerged in the juvenile court—an equilibrium which, like most others, is best defined as a cozy arrangement maintained at the expense of those without the capacity to disturb it.

That the kadi is satisfied with this cozy arrangement requires little further explication. In an important sense, the emergent equilibrium was put together to rescue him from the free-floating good will of his authoritative predecessors and contemporary underlings. In presenting the contours of the emergent amalgam, I have already suggested the ways in which it meets the needs of the kadi. But what of his underlings? In what ways are the needs of the more or less social-work-oriented probation officers met by the cozy arrangement? The answer is not too difficult, and fortunately one need not invoke the embarrassing matter of professional imperialism even though it is occasionally apparent. The main answer lies in the way in which the probation workers are themselves mystified by the very system they have strived to create. Like many underlings they do not fully understand the workings of their system. They characteristically and necessarily see it from their own perspective.

Probation workers, with the important exception of those whose eventual fate is to leave the system, a typical way of maintaining equilibrium, normally believe that the system works in furthering *their* goals of mercy and rehabilitation. The traces of rampant error are easily obscured by frequent reference to the need for more and more staff, implying that with more, better-trained, and better-paid personnel the delinquency problem could be better handled, and by the equally frequent humble concession that more and more knowledge about the etiology of delinquents is required—what we need is more research. Thus, there is no necessity that rampant failure be taken as a reflection of the system. The system simply suffers from remediable defects in personnel and knowledge—what system does not? That defect noted, and more or less accounted for, the probation worker may continue to conceive of the ways in which the juvenile court system furthers his goals of mercy and rehabilitation. How may he do this? First, he may observe that the overwhelming majority of actual cases are rendered unto him and *not* to prison. In this reckoning he is undoubtedly right. A variable but always small proportion of cases culminate in incarceration. The great majority of juveniles are regularly put on some manner of probation many times before actual incarceration occurs. When the day of ultimate juvenile judgment finally occurs, when the judge is to render the juvenile unto prison, the probation worker is likely to agree with his kadi. He may even anticipate him and initiate the recommendation. By this time he agrees that he "can't help that child." Moreover, the increasing use of social workers and their rhetoric within the prison establishment allows the probation worker to believe that the child now is simply being referred to another specialist in help who happens to have his office in residential settings called "training homes," "vocational institutes," "work farms," or simply "cottages." His training in mystification has allowed him to obscure from himself and others the essence of the whole system. It is a system which, especially in its residential form, prison, but also in its out-patient setting, probation, deals incessantly in *penal sanctions*. Other things may happen also but it does no good to deny a process its essence. To deny a process its essence is the deepest meaning of mystification.

Francis Allen, who is in many ways the most incisive commentator on socialized justice suggests:

There is one proposition which, if generally understood, would contribute more to clear thinking on these matters than any other. It is not a new insight. Seventy years ago, the Italian criminologist Garofalo asserted: "The mere deprivation of liberty, however benign the administration of the place of confinement, is undeniable punishment." This proposition may be rephrased as follows: Measures which subject individuals to the substantial and involuntary deprivation of liberty are essentially punitive in character, and this reality is not altered by the fact that the motivations that prompt incarceration are to provide therapy or otherwise contribute to the person's well-being or reform.[27]

Thus, the probation worker's training, the fact that the great majority of juvenile cases are rendered to him rather than prison, the fact that by the time the juvenile is incarcerated the probation worker is willing to grant that he cannot help him, and the fact that other professional helpers have now become ensconced in prisons, allows him to be satisfied with a system that dispenses not mercy but a special form of penal sanction. His need to believe himself a professional trained in the arts of mercy, understanding, and rehabilitation are met.

Finally, the tacit reinstituting of a principle of offense is obscured from him. My impression is that few probation workers would agree that such reinstituting has occurred. The principle of offense has been and is a central target of probation and social-work hostility, and for good reason. It denies them their calling in court. But, as mentioned, that is not the main reason they oppose the principle of offense and that is not why they would disagree with the assertion that it has been reinstituted. They deny its propriety because by inclination and training they are convinced that it is morally wrong and clinically contraindicated. They deny its reinstitution either because they are right—it has not been reinstituted—in which case I am wrong, or because they have been mystified by court rhetoric into believing that the basis of disposition is individualized justice and not the amalgam of a principle of offense tempered by a primary doctrine of parental sponsorship and a secondary doctrine of residential availability.

Empirically, we cannot be sure which alternative to choose. It is simply my impression against theirs. The obvious means of resolution—more research which is at any rate always needed—is not so easy to come by or design. It is exceedingly difficult to learn with certainty the bases for decision in any court. It is especially difficult in a court bestowed with great discretion and given to flowery rhetoric. The basis for my claim, and it is obviously little more than that, is a bit of observation, some intuition, and the theoretical argument that workaday systems develop codes that operationalize initially vague principles.

Let us proceed on the assumption that my description of the emergent basis for disposition is correct. Let he who makes different assessments develop his own argument. If I am right then the probation worker's misconception of the workings of his system are consequential. His misconception serves to further commit him to the cozy arrangement. The inherent difficulties in discerning the bases of the kadi's disposition, and the kadi's practiced art of rendering all dispositions in the rhetoric of individualized judgment and treatment serve to mystify the underlings in that system. From their perspective it appears as if the kadi has maintained *their* moral and clinical objections to the principle of offense. Indeed, my point has been that it appears that way from almost everyone's, including the kadi's, perspective. The reinstituting of the principle of offense has been obscured from almost everyone. It has been obscured from every perspective save one: the jaundiced perspective of a few cynical juvenile delinquents who regularly receive the justice of the juvenile court. The great majority of juvenile delinquents have little talent in analysis. They simply accept the analytic conclusions arrived at by the very few theorists among them. What I have attempted to do is to develop through observation and intuition the jaundiced viewpoints expressed to me by those very few delinquents who are articulate regarding these matters. Though I do not believe that I have been led astray by these informants, it would be ungrateful of me to disclaim their initial guidance.

How do the workings of this arrangement appear to juvenile delinquents? The answer may be simply stated. It appears unjust —rampantly so. Few delinquents can do more than express a simmering sense of injustice. They cannot explain why they sense injustice. That is our job. They cannot explain it partly because they are half-literate schoolboys, but mainly because they, like everyone else, are mystified by what goes on in court. In some ways they are even more mystified. In addition to the normal sources of mystification, the juvenile delinquent is additionally confused because, unfortunately, he hardly understands most of the words that are used in court. Like Camus' stranger, he is frequently a mystified observer at his own trial. But he is aware of the outcome, the disposition. He hears the disposition and he hears and partly understands the words that are used to justify that disposition. In other words, he hears that he is either being put on probation or in prison and that the reason in both cases is to help him. That is about all that he really hears in court. It is quite enough.

The little that he hears and understands in court is enough to maintain and refuel the delinquent's sense of injustice. Because of the structure of the court, its mysteries and its rhetoric, the accused cannot see the actual consistency implicit in the emergent amalgam that guides disposition. The subcultural delinquent senses rampant inconsistency because he sees the workings of that system out of context. This is no ordinary taking out of context. It is an enormous misconception in which *doctrines are confused with principles.* For this enormous misconception, he must be pardoned. He is not alone in seeing the juvenile court out of context. Since one of its normal features is mystification, almost everyone who serves the system, passes through it, or observes it is encouraged to mistake its workings. Everyone is encouraged to believe that the basis of disposition is individualized justice. Thus, whenever a glimmering appears that this is not a basis for decision, the stage is set for the imputation of hypocrisy, favoritism, or whimsical inconsistency.

Hypocrisy is imputed if the recipient of justice simply dismisses the official explanation for disposition as pious cant. Favoritism is imputed by more theoretically inclined delinquents. For this kind of subcultural delinquent, the suspicion that he is being misled regarding the basis of disposition suggests the necessity of exploratory speculation regarding the true bases. Why should persons so important and influential as the judge and his helpers lie to him regarding the true bases of disposition? Why should they insist, as they frequently do, that it is not what he did—which strikes delinquents and others as a sensible reason for legal intervention—but his underlying problems and difficulties that guide court action? Why do they say they are helping him when patently they are limiting his freedom of action and movement by putting him on probation or in prison? What on earth could they possibly be hiding that would lead them to such heights of deception?

Once engaged in this line of speculation, a theory stressing favoritism suggests itself. It is not only suggested by the presumptions of the subculture, which at any rate must have origins if subculture is to be anything more than a question-begging concept. Favoritism is suggested to the delinquent and to his subculture by the glimmering of the two doctrinal qualifications used by the court in tempering the principle of offense. Recall, the kadi and his helpers publicly deny the principle of offense in the presence of delinquents. If the delinquent simply ignores these disclaimers, then he may challenge the competence of the court. It lies. It is hypocritical. But if delinquents believe the disclaimers regarding the principle of offense, then they take their hints as the court presents them. The doctrinal qualifications of parental sponsorship and residential availability are persistently cued. The delinquent, forced as he is by the disclaimer regarding the principle of offense, takes the doctrines completely out of context. He is inadvertently encouraged to mistake the doctrinal qualifications for guiding principles! For him, as for sociologists who have made the identical mistake, the stage is prepared for the accusation of rank favoritism and inconsistency.

If the principle of offense is disclaimed by officials and subsequently discounted by delinquents, and if, instead, the doctrines of parental sponsorship and residential availability are mistaken for principles of disposition, the situation becomes ludicrous. The mistaken principles are obviously unfair, *from everyone's point of view*. As doctrines, parental sponsorship and residential availability are at least debatable, at best quite sensible. As principles, they are at best indefensible, at worst, utterly scandalous.

One has to understand what it would mean if parental sponsorship and residential availability were themselves principles instead of doctrinal qualifications of a principle of offense in order to appreciate the scandalous implications of such an unlikely state of affairs. It would mean, for instance, that, *with little or no regard for the offense or prior record,* troubled boys whose parents could afford the kind of sponsorship entailed in private therapy should be disposed of differently than those whose parents could hardly afford such sponsorship. It would mean that, *with little or no regard for the offense or prior record,* boys with no parents or negligent parents should go to prison whereas those with earnest parents should be put on probation. Nobody would defend parental sponsorship as a principle guiding disposition, not even court agents. Such a state of affairs would as much smack of favoritism to them as to delinquents. Consequently, the kadi and his helpers face a problem in justifying a decision whenever an explanation is requested by one of their juvenile clients. They attempt to justify and interpret dispositions on the basis of the individual needs of the offender. Since they seek to avoid an explanation resting on the principle of offense, since they cannot justify parental sponsorship or residential availability as principles, and since they are unaware of their status as doctrines, they are likely to engage in *ad hoc* justifications. They try, like the professor justifying a grade on a highly subjective essay examination to an irate student, to be as convincing as possible, to use any argument that seems satisfying. Like all such *ad hoc* justifications, the traces of whimsical inconsistency are clear and apparent, *especially* if two or more clients should happen to engage in mutually enlightening conversation. The court agent, as a last resort, may attempt to convince the juvenile that each case is a separate matter and differently handled. The agent may suggest that the juvenile should not compare himself to others, that that is part of his problem. It is. The concern with justice taken as consistency is a problem for all of us. It inexorably converts us into busybodies.

Even if it is possible for juveniles to mistake the primary doctrine of parental sponsorship for a principle, could they possibly be goaded to the same sort of error regarding the secondary doctrine of residential availability? Such a conception seems possible though probably it does not occur as frequently as the mistaking of the doctrine of parental sponsorship for a principle. Occasionally, however, delinquents will surmise that "it's not what you do that matters, but whether there's room for you some place." One delinquent put it this way:

In the children's court, I had found, there are two kinds of judges: bleeding hearts and swords of the Lord. Bleeding hearts called me son and wept over me; swords of the Lord shouted I ought to be locked up in a zoo. But I thought there was no real difference between the two. If there was room for you in the slammers, either kind sent you up. Usually there was no room. That is why I got off with a warning the twelve times before this.[28]

Thus, the incredible seems possible. Because of the structure and rhetoric of the juvenile court, subcultural delinquents passing through it are inadvertently stimulated to mistake doctrines for principles. Consequently, they discern inconsistency in the form of hypocrisy, favoritism, and whimsy. This, despite the fact that the juvenile court, in shaping a new amalgam which guides its dispositions, has managed to develop considerable consistency in its procedures and decisions. The misunderstandings implicit in this process are a direct consequence of the mystery that characterizes the structure of the court and the mystification that is featured in its rhetoric.

Though the sense of injustice is felt most keenly when we are made to suffer, the observation that we can benefit from injustice is not without consequence. Delinquents talk to one another. The concern with consistency results in an interest in other people's business. Since consistency is a comparative concept, there is no other way than snooping to assess the measure in which it appears. For every case in which a delinquent has been the victim of what he takes to be inconsistency, there are other cases in which he has been the beneficiary. Tales of "bum raps" are more than matched by those of "beating raps." Thus, it is clear that the subculture of delinquency does not simply overlook or ignore the benefits of injustice. But neither does it simply accept both faces of injustice and stoically reason that such things have a way of balancing each other out in the long run. Such a view would be markedly inconsistent with the general stance taken by subcultural delinquents toward the agents of law enforcement. The logic of subcultural delinquency turns *both* the sufferance and the benefit into indictments of the system. Suffering an injustice may be seen as a violation of many components of justice—cognizance, consistency, and the rest. Indictments due to benefits derived from injustice are founded on discrediting the *competence* of the official system.

Competence

It is only fair that you who pass judgment on me sustain the right to do so. Not everyone is entitled to pass judgment. The refrain "who are *you* to sit in judgment over me" is a familiar one. Competence is not an issue only among delinquents. It is probably a universal component of the sense of justice. The process of judgment can hardly appear in communal life without simultaneous regard for the credentials of those who presume to evaluate. Judgment is always in some measure a presumption of superior status. Consequently, the recipient of judgment may exercise the option of inquiring into the authenticity of the presumed superiority. The inquiry into authenticity may result in honoring or dishonoring the credentials of those who presume to sit in judgment.

From the conventional viewpoint, such credentials are *formally* implicit in certain statuses. Judges, probation officers, policemen, parents, teachers, and others have a community license to sit in judgment. But the holding of a formal license is not enough—not among those who because of their curious symbiotic relation to instituted authority come to patrol the activities of their masters. Like servants, juvenile delinquents have a special interest and strategic access to the affairs of their masters. Ascriptive license or yesterday's achieved license may suffice for the general community but not for those who are tended by instituted authority. For them, the credentials on which license for judgment are based undergo regular scrutiny. *Their* court is always in session.

Thus, those who are regularly judged come to sit in judgment over instituted authority. They do this illicitly since they possess no communal license for such an endeavor, but they do so nonetheless. Indeed, the consequence of their lack of license is not a forestalling of such activities; instead, unlicensed judgment, like most forms of unlicensed activities, merely results in an irresponsible and untrammeled version of the conventional counterpart. Licensed activities are more restricted and more responsible than unlicensed counterparts. Licensed judgment is guarded. The judgment of unlicensed underlings is likely to result in harsh, demanding, and unjust verdicts.

Given the special interest and special access to official activity implicit in his relations with instituted authority, and the unlicensed character of judgment, one might expect that the subcultural delinquent's assessment regarding official competence would be universally negative. Such is not the case. Fine discriminations are made among those who man each of the official systems—police, court, school, social work, ministry—with which the delinquent maintains an ongoing if sporadic contact. Though their judgment is without license it is not completely without reason. There is no necessity to dishonor the credentials of all or even a majority of officials.

Since the subculture of delinquency collects examples of incompetence on a variety of grounds, it may sustain the sense of rampant official violation and thus injustice through the *economic* use of relatively few cases. Thus, a question put to delinquents regarding their opinion of the proportion of discredited officials misses the point. It reckons without the hoarding propensities that characterize subcultural economies. Thus, the subcultural delinquent may exhibit discrimination and apparently reasoned judgment in conceding that many or even most officials are competent and still maintain a sense of injustice resting on a *general* discrediting of officialdom on grounds of incompetence. This intellectual sleight-of-hand is by no means unusual. Any bigot will concede that there are a few or even lots of good Negroes or Mexicans. Stereotyping does not rest on statistical statements regarding the frequency of discredited members of a category. It rests on the *avoidance* of statistical reasoning which can easily be maintained in many milieus except for those extremely rare and inconsequential occasions when an interloping interviewer momentarily introduces the respondent to statistical reasoning.

Thus, the subcultural delinquent is of two minds regarding the credentials of instituted authorities. On the one hand, he engages in a general discrediting of authorities which culminates in an overall verdict of incompetence on a variety of grounds. On the other hand, he discriminates, judging each member of officialdom on his or her individual merits.[29] Depending on mood and context, he will display one or the other mind. Our main concern is with the judgments he makes during unkind moods. It is on those occasions that he proclaims the incompetence of his official over-seers.

There are two grounds on which the competence of those who sit in judgment is itself judged. The subcultural delinquent, like the rest of us, wishes to know about the *piety*, or moral compe-tence, and the *effectiveness*, or technical competence, of those who judge. Though his interests are similar to those of the general public, his curiosity is greater. The subjects of persistent judgment —the delinquent is surely one—reciprocate the interest. They reckon that one who is so interested in them must himself be a rather interesting character. Like the subjects of psychotherapy, they become busybodies—aspirant experts in the character of their caretakers. It is in this sense that the delinquent has a special interest in the competence of instituted authorities. His *special interest*, strategic access or *special perspective*, and unlicensed position or *special status* inhere in the structure of the delinquent's relations with officials. Because of these special qualities, the sub-cultural delinquent's judgments regarding the piety and effective-ness of officials are likely to take forms that appear strange and distorted when compared to the allegedly more objective view-point of conventional persons. People with special interests, special perspective and special status are by definition precluded from the possibility of objective judgment. Thus, the delinquent's view of officials is intensely subjective. Whether anyone else's view is less subjective is a moot point. Be that as it may, it is the subjective view of the delinquent that I wish to make explicit.

Piety

Our expectations regarding piety depend partly on the airs taken by persons. It is fitting social vengeance to maintain more demanding standards of piety for those who by their actions presume moral superiority than for those who are more humble in their claims. Judgments are made by delinquents regarding the piety of the officials who oversee them. The propriety of their conduct is evaluated more stringently and more demandingly than that of ordinary folk. Officials, by their actions, presume higher moral attainments. The presumption of moral superiority is deeply imbedded in the work of all officials who oversee delinquents. This presumption may be latent in official operation and never receive expression, or it may appear patently in explicit utterances or "preaching." This presumption, common to all overseer offices, and not the unreasoned character of delinquent thought, lies behind the double standard by which delinquents may expect considerably more of their official overseers than their overseers of them. The official legal standards set for juveniles are *minimal* though they are not as low as those set for adults. The customary delinquent standards set for officials are *maximal* though not as high for some officials as others.

The official may be suspected, accused, or indicted for deviation from the norms of piety. The rapidity with which such suspicions may culminate in indictment surpass anything found even in juvenile court. Underlying the rapidity of verdict is a procedural laxity far surpassing anything found in licensed judgment. Not only is hearsay evidence permissible, it is universally prevalent. No one bothers to check out stories. They are taken at their word. Heated denials rendered by officials are likely to be taken as signs of protesting too much and thus may elicit further defamation. There is no machinery by which the character of officials may be protected from defamation. If the judgmental system prevalent in the juvenile court is a bureaucratic version of *kadi* justice, then the system prevalent among delinquents is a vulgar rendition of *poetic* justice. The poetic justice rendered by delinquents to their overseer officials, like all forms of poetic justice, is a fitting or foreseeable travesty of the real thing. It is a travesty because poetic justice is never terribly just in anything but the poetic sense of the term. It is fitting or foreseeable because it is a parody on the perceived shortcomings of the juvenile justice received by the delinquent.

The system of justice by which delinquents evaluate officials is a Coney Island mirror image of the system by which officials evaluate them.[30] The procedural laxity of juvenile justice is aped by delinquents and surpassed in a manner that could only be attained by sardonic and half-literate schoolboys. The raising of the minimal expectations characteristic of criminal law in the juvenile jurisdictions [31] are aped and surpassed in the maintaining of *maximal* standards in the evaluation of official piety. And, finally, as in all Coney Island mirrors, the major sanction held by the mirror image is mockery, ridicule, and scorn. No matter how we ridicule or mock or scorn the image in the mirror, it surpasses us. The image is a grotesque reflection of unwanted tendencies in our own selves. We may eventually crush the mirror, walk away from it, or good-humoredly surrender to it, but we may never outmock it. That is the essential and sometimes the sole sanction possessed by social types who approach the image in the mirror with respect to their power, autonomy, and inventiveness.

The subcultural delinquent cannot imprison officials or put them on probation, and only rarely does he resort to corporal punishment; but he can ridicule and scorn them and thus make a mockery of their work and career. For officials, this is no mean sanction. Judgments of the piety of officials are made with few procedural safeguards. Virtually any loudly proclaimed accusation is honored. No documentation is necessary. The sanctions for indictments of turpitude are mockery, ridicule, and scorn with the consequence of regular interference with the work and thus the career of the official. These points require little elaboration; however, the point about the application of maximal standards does. Because of the appearance of maximal standards, there are many opportunities for accusation, indictment, and sanctioning of officials.

The standards applied to officials by subcultural delinquents are maximal. Special considerations applicable only to officials are added to the standards applied to all citizens. This is a double standard in the fullest sense since the standard is not only different; it is higher in that it includes the less stringent demands. It is a double standard in almost the same sense in which juveniles are subjected to a double standard. One consequence of the sense of injustice evoked by a perceived double standard is to withdraw approval and question the legitimacy of law. The other consequence is to reciprocate and apply an analogous double standard to those who seemingly perpetrate the injustice. The subculture of delinquency is pervaded by both responses.

Conventional citizens also hold higher expectations of overseer officials than of themselves, but not with the same sense of insistent urgency displayed by subcultural delinquents. The urgent application of a double standard is regularly reserved for those communal officials who oversee *us*. The mark of insistent urgency is vigilant scrutiny. The most persistently vigilant scrutinizers of police, court, educational and social-work officials are not conventional citizens or even investigatory specialists. They are the subjects of official surveillance—in this case, juvenile delinquents. We, the conventional citizens, have other morally superior overseers who occupy our attention.

Thus, for conventional folk, the higher expectations held of delinquency-control officials are present but largely unattended. We may gullibly assume that these high standards are by and large met, or cynically assume that they are by and large violated, but in either case the matter is not, strictly speaking, our business. It understandably fails to preoccupy us. The matter does preoccupy subcultural delinquents, and that preoccupation distinguishes their assertion of maximal standards for officials from the superficially similar assertion of conventional folk.

The official overseers of juvenile delinquents may display moral turpitude by violating norms that apply to all of us—*the norms of citizenship;* by violating special norms that apply to their positions—*the duties of office;* and by illicitly transcending the perquisites allowed their office—*forgetting their place.* Each violation may be commemorated in subcultural annals. Each instance is an occasion for challenging the competence of instituted authority. Each is a way in which the delinquent's sense of injustice is refurbished, refueled, and reinforced by conventional society.

The norms of citizenship are, at first glance, rarely violated by officials. If these were the only norms applicable to the officials who oversee delinquents, the subculture of delinquency would apparently be forced to economizing ventures bordering on austerity. Even in Chicago, where police and court violations of the duties of office have been commonplace for a century, the commission of a series of grand thefts and burglaries by a ring of policemen in 1960 was so incredible a spectacle as to elicit a major scandal in that normally jaded city.

Tacitly, at least, the normal run of police derelictions, ranging from corruption to brutality, have come to be treated as violations of duty of office. Even though many of these acts of corruption or brutality may technically be treated as crimes, elicit penal sanctions, and thus qualify as violations of the norms of citizenship, the normal response to these acts is discharge, transfer, or demotion—sanctions that attach themselves to violations of the duties of office. Thus, by administrative custom, most ordinary police violations have come to be treated as breaches of official capacity. But while I—a sociological observer with the generosity and disinterest of all unconcerned outsiders—am satisfied with simply stating that *de facto* practice transforms *de jure* principles, it would be indeed surprising if the subcultural delinquent with his special interest and special perspective arrived at quite the same statement.

The subculture of delinquency avoids an economizing program bordering on austerity by insisting in the face of contrary custom that policemen who are involved in corruption, brutality, and other endeavors that are technically violations of minimal norms of citizenship are *just like criminals,* only worse because they are additionally guilty of fraud. Thus, the conventional Chicagoan's reactions to the scandalous enormity of police-led burglary rings was not duplicated in the world of subcultural delinquency. There, it was taken in stride, though with relish. To them, this was the way in which the police can be expected to behave, not because they claimed that police traditionally engaged in burglary but because burglary was of a piece with regular police violations. It was continuous with the crime of accessory which is implicit in every act of corruption and the crime of assault implicit in every act of brutality.

Not all or even most policemen, not even perhaps in Chicago, commit crimes. But everywhere, some do. Thus, while the subculture of delinquency must economize, the strained stretching of a very few morsels—austerity—hardly seems necessary. There are sufficient instances of unconfirmed criminal violations by officials—procedural laxity makes confirmation unnecessary—to allow the normal economizing mechanisms of a subculture to produce a sense of rampant official turpitude.

If, as delinquents and the law insist, corruption, brutality, and similar endeavors are not, as is customarily held, mere violations of office but violations of the minimal norms of citizenship—crimes—then what sorts of action properly qualify as violations of official duty? There are many kinds of violation of office. Most are of little interest here. A few seem pertinent because they are most directly visible to delinquents. Obviously, only those derelictions of duty directly visible attain infamy in the subculture of delinquency.

With the exception of judge, all of the offices that regularly oversee the conduct of juveniles share a single overriding characteristic. They are all *marginal professions*.[32] Teaching, social work, probation and law enforcement are all aspirant professions that lack one or more of the ordinary social bases of respect from which self-styled professions receive public confirmation. Professions derive respect from the performance of tasks that are publicly acknowledged as vital and difficult, from their publicly acknowledged high social standing as manifested in high salary or prestige, or from the hallowed character of the office as evidenced in traditional public imputations of extraordinary or sacred character. Thus, there are actually only a few secure or accomplished professions in the United States, the majority being aspirant and marginal professions. Overseer occupations, with the exception of judge, are marginal professions with the additional misfortune of working with a clientele that patrols their activities. Secure professions such as doctor, lawyer, judge, professor, minister, and perhaps scientist share the characteristic of having already accomplished the major hurdle of professional identity—a stable synthesis of the ordinarily antithetical ideas implicit in the concepts of *calling* and *job*. A stable synthesis of these ordinarily conflicting ideas is no easy accomplishment. Consequently, it usually takes many centuries before aspirant professions become secure. During the period of professional purgatory, occupations and their incumbents normally vacillate between the ideas implicit in the concepts of calling and job instead of synthesizing them. Marginal professions, like any marginal entity, are uncertain of their place. They exhibit their uncertainty by vacillating. Furthermore, they vacillate between exaggerated or overdrawn versions of both calling and job.

The derelictions of duty that are most directly visible to subcultural delinquents, and thus those on which I wish to focus, are connected to the vacillation between calling and job, manifested by overseer officials. My thesis is that delinquents infer considerable moral and technical incompetence from the vacillation they observe.

The vacillation between the conception of calling and that of job exposes officials to claims which in a variety of ways inpugn their character. Because officials vacillate, subcultural delinquents who patrol their behavior may have it both ways. Officials may be accused of incompetence on occasions when they seemingly stress the conception of calling and, also, when they stress the conception of job. When officials act as if their marginal profession were a calling, the subcultural delinquent may remind them of the sense in which it is merely a job. When officials act as if it were merely a job, the subcultural delinquent may remind them of the sense in which it is supposed to be a calling.

A calling is a moral vocation carrying with it extraordinary obligations and prerequisites. A job is just that—a job. It is mundane. Its obligations and rights are ordinary. Among the extraordinary obligations of a calling is a tenacious dedication to one's flock, a noble eschewing of considerations of career, an indifference to the matters of hours worked, conditions of work, and salary, and a deep and publicized belief in the joy of one's vocation. Among the perquisites of such lofty office is the right to explicitly flaunt through verbal pronouncements the sentiments and purpose that underlie the moral superiority of those who work at callings. Those who work at callings are permitted to *preach*. Judges, clergymen, professors, doctors, and perhaps lawyers and scientists are allowed to flaunt their moral superiority.[33] In a sense, each is expected to engage in frequent pontificating. When officials working at marginal professions engage in frequent pontificating and in explicit flaunting of moral superiority, as they sometimes do, the audience is not as likely to indulge them that privilege. Such officials, by their admission on other occasions, are simply working at jobs like anyone else. When officials in marginal professions preach, the term "preach" is likely to be used in a derogatory and sardonic way.[34] Preaching is not their perquisite. Instead, it is taken as a sign that the incumbent has forgotten his place or, rather, that he has forgotten the place of his office.

To forget one's place is a moral affront. It is an act of minor impiety, but one that is particularly open to mockery, ridicule, and scorn. Mockery, ridicule, and scorn are especially appropriate sanctions when the deviation is one of taking on airs. Subcultural delinquents have a special competence in the barbed deflating of pretensions. Their favorite activity—sounding—gives them a special competence in such pursuits. Thus, the special vulnerability of marginal professions and the special competence of subcultural delinquents combine in a manner that enhances the possibilities of frequent derogation and defamation. Whenever a policeman, social worker, probation officer, or teacher flaunts his moral superiority—whenever he preaches—and thus stresses the conception of his work as a calling, he exposes himself to a reminder that he is after all simply working at a job. He may be put back in his place. Incumbents of marginal professions who are given to preaching are likely to be known as "pricks" or some more up-to-date equivalent. They are subjected to frequent mockery because by their actions they have revealed themselves as persons who take on airs. They are given to extraordinary posture but occupy an ordinary position.

Just as the marginal professional vacillates, so too does the subcultural delinquent. The trouble is that delinquents' vacillation is contracyclical. His mission is to constantly remind the official of his other self-conception.

Officials frequently seek to impress their charges with the fact that they are, like anyone else, simply doing their job. They may do this either as a clinical tactic in the belief that delinquents can be reached by stressing down-to-earth matters, or because they sincerely happen to feel that way on many occasions. Though this sort of modesty sometimes elicits sympathy or cooperation, it may also elicit a sharp reminder of the greater expectations implicit in their office. Moreover, officials may often betray the sense in which their jobs are just jobs. They do this in many ways, each contaminating central aspects of the conception of calling. They cannot go too far out on a limb for a client, thus falling considerably short of the tenacious dedication to one's flock implicit in a conception of calling. They take and may publicly seek better jobs and thus not eschew considerations of career as is expected of those with callings. They publicly, and sometimes endlessly, complain of low salary, poor working conditions, and long hours, and thus betray anything but the obligatory indifference to such matters of those in callings. Simultaneously, they inadvertently show that their conception of work is far from joyous, thus violating the final expectation of those who work· at callings.

When officials by their words and actions stress the sense in which their jobs are just jobs, they open themselves to the charge of hypocrisy. They become known as "pork-choppers," or some more up-to-date equivalent. Because of their vacillation, and the contracyclical vacillation of the subcultural delinquents, they are on these occasions seen as mundane occupants of extraordinary positions. By the nature of their matter-of-fact and down to earth attitude, they have profaned a hallowed calling. The subcultural delinquent, because he is engaged in unlicensed judgment, may often have it both ways. In this particular case, however, he surpasses his ordinary capacities. He may have it a third way, too. He may take the conception of office as simply a job and convert it to the opening indictment of official lack of technical competence.

Ineffectiveness

If social work, probation, teaching, and police work are jobs, they are certainly not very good ones. Anyone in our society knows that, especially subcultural delinquents. If they do not know it from other sources, they learn about it directly from their overseers. Official overseers regularly tell their charges that they are overworked, underpaid, and in other ways unappreciated. The subcultural delinquent need not wholly believe the sad status tales told by the overseer officials. Sometimes he may take them to be the normal complaints of any task, sometimes he may see them as self-serving claims of persons who by his standards have a well-paid and easy job, *but* sometimes he may take them as confessions indicative of personal incompetence. When he takes the sad tales as confessions, he may reason that persons who are driven to such unrewarding and ungratifying positions must themselves possess personal shortcomings. Otherwise, they might have attained more lucrative or prestigeful positions. The idea or even the glimmering that those who man overseer positions possess little talent is an extremely corrosive one since it brings into question the quality of whatever service officials claim to be dis-

pensing. Thus, a *prima facie* case may be made for the ineffectiveness of the delinquency-control system. Such a case can be made
without the necessity of further documentation or evidence of
official ineffectiveness. Officials may be assumed ineffective by
subcultural delinquents simply on the face of it since they would
hardly have gravitated to such unappreciated work if they were
effective persons. The status of an office may be taken as a sign
of the talent of the incumbent. This is a common idea and not one
limited to delinquents.

The subcultural delinquent could rest his indictment of ineffectiveness on this *prima facie* case. His judgment is unlicensed.
Thus, he is under no sustained obligation to augment his *prima
facie* case for the personal incompetence of overseer officials. However, the additional evidence is so easy to come by that it would
be foolish to base the indictment of ineffectiveness on an assumption. Subcultural delinquents possess a tremendous amount of
evidence regarding the ineffectiveness of overseer officials. The
evidence is inherent in the multitude of public offenses, known to
subcultural adherents, but hardly public or known by the official
overseers. Obviously, there are a great many offenses for which
the culprit remains undetected. The fact that most of the subcultural delinquent's offenses go undetected and, furthermore,
the fact that at least a few of his colleagues continuously evade
apprehension is taken as an unmistakable sign of official ineffectiveness. Any one of the thousands of undetected offenses can
be presented as documentation or evidence of rampant official ineffectiveness. Almost every adherent of subcultural delinquency
"gets away" with many offenses.

Futher evidence of official ineffectiveness is presented in the
continuous subcultural hearings on official incompetence. The
police inability to capture the culprit in most offenses is only a
piece of evidence. In addition, subcultural testimony is developed
regarding the relative ease with which officials may be outwitted,
outmaneuvered, or otherwise "conned" in the event of apprehension. Subcultural delinquents not only "get away" with lots of
things. They frequently speak of the many "raps" they have
"beaten." Public boasts of outsmarting officials is the way in which
testimony in the subcultural hearings is given. Boasting, bragging,
and bravado are continuous features of the subcultural round of

activity. They are the other side of sounding. Boasting is an un-solicited assertion of one's own capacity and depth. As such, boasting is continuous and consistent with a central activity of delinquent life—sounding. A consequence of the prominence of boasting, and the forms taken by it, is the regular derogation of official effectiveness.

The official system is subjected to one final charge. It is a momentous charge and serves as a capstone for the entire indict-ment of official injustice. Once rampant ineffectiveness of officials is demonstrated to the satisfaction of subcultural adherents, a monstrous and incredible injustice gradually comes to mind. If officials are extremely ineffective, could it not perhaps be that *everybody commits many offenses* and only a few suffer the mis-fortune of apprehension? Many, including a few of the delin-quents' colleagues, escape apprehension. Once apprehended, of-ficial cognizance is focused and the chances of subsequent ap-prehension maximized. This possibility—and it is taken as no more than a possibility—is the darkest suspicion of subcultural delinquency and the most profound basis for its sense of injustice.

In this chapter, I have tried to suggest a variety of ways in which the subcultural delinquent senses injustice. His sense of injustice develops within the conducive context of contemporary juvenile justice. This context does not cause the sense of injustice but it helps sustain it. I have focused on three components of justice: cognizance, consistency, and competence. In the follow-ing chapter, I turn to the remaining components: commensurabil-ity and comparison.

NOTES

1. For a systematic elaboration of this point, see H. L. A. Hart, *The Con-cept of Law*, Oxford, England: Clarendon Press, 1961, Chaps. 1–4.
2. For an interesting discussion of injustice different from that which will be elaborated here, see Richard Cloward and Lloyd Ohlin, *Delinquency and Opportunity*, Glencoe, Ill.: Free Press, 1960, pp. 113–124. Cloward and Ohlin focus on the sense of *social injustice*—the way in which social inequities contribute to the delinquent's alienation and resentment. My focus will be on *legal injustice*.
3. Injustice-collecting seems to be a general feature of deviant subcultures. For a discussion of injustice-collecting among homosexuals, for instance,

see Hervey Cleckley, *The Caricature of Love,* New York: Ronald Press, 1957.

4. Paul W. Tappan, "Who is the Criminal?," *American Sociological Review,* February 1947, p. 160.

5. Edwin H. Sutherland and Donald R. Cressey, *Principles of Criminology,* sixth edition, Philadelphia: Lippincott, 1960, pp. 18–19.

6. Hart, *op. cit.,* p. 154.

7. *Ibid.,* pp. 153–154.

8. Allen Barton and Saul Mendlovitz, "The Experience of Injustice as a Research Problem," *Journal of Legal Education,* Vol. 13, No. 1, p. 24.

9. Hart, *op. cit.,* p. 154.

10. Barton and Mendlovitz, *loc. cit.*

11. This formulation is similar to that implicit in Edmund N. Cahn, *The Sense of Injustice,* New York: New York University Press, 1949, pp. 12–21.

12. For an excellent general discussion of police discretion, see Joseph Goldstein, "Police Discretion Not to Invoke the Criminal Process: Low Visibility Decisions in the Administration of Justice," *Yale Law Journal,* March 1960, pp. 543–594.

13. Ira H. Freeman, *Out of the Burning: The Story of a Boy Gang Leader,* New York: Crown, 1960, p. 175.

14. *Ibid.,* p. 176.

15. *Ibid.*

16. Hart. *op. cit.,* p. 102.

17. Cahn, *op. cit.,* pp. 14–15.

18. The following discussion is based on the literature on juvenile courts, on intensive observation of juvenile courts over a period of three months in 1960–61, and intermittent observation since then.

19. See, for instance, Gustav L. Schramm, "Philosophy of Juvenile Court," *Annals of the American Academy of Political and Social Science,* January 1949, pp. 101–108; Roscoe Pound, "The Rise of Socialized Criminal Justice," *National Probation Association Yearbook,* 1942, pp. 1–22; Edward F. Waite, "How Far Can Court Procedures Be Socialized without Impairing Individual Rights?," *Journal of Criminal Law and Criminology,* November 1921, pp. 339–347; Alfred J. Kahn, *A Court for Children,* New York: Columbia University Press, 1943.

20. The question of the tenability of the categoric status distinctions separating juvenile from adult jurisdictions will be taken up in Chapter 5.

21. See, for instance, *Guides for Juvenile Court Judges,* New York: Advisory Council of Judges of the National Probation and Parole Association, in cooperation with the National Council of Juvenile Court Judges, 1957.

22. That qualification is important. Some juvenile courts explicitly deny the modern enlightened canons and, instead, subscribe to the idea that legalistic notions stressing the principle of offense should be adhered to. My impression is that such courts are few and far between; but whatever their number, the present discussion has little bearing on them.

23. Max Rheinstein (editor), *Max Weber on Law in Economy and Society,*

Cambridge, Mass.: Harvard University Press, 1954, p. xlvii. Translation from Max Weber, *Wirtschaft and Gesellschaft*, by Edward Shils and Max Rheinstein.

24. *Ibid.*, p. 216.

25. *Ibid.*

26. Neither of these generalizations is negated by the accurate and acute observations that ethically or self-imposed limitations may in fact limit the discretion of the kadi, that informal organization may in fact widen the discretion of bureaucratic officials, and that the higher one's place in a bureaucracy the greater his discretionary power. These are all true, as has been attested to either directly or indirectly in sociological theory and research. However, they are in the nature of important doctrinal qualifications of the main sociological principles which suggest that, *in the main,* kadi maximizes discretion, whereas bureaucracy minimizes it.

27. Francis A. Allen, "Criminal Justice and the Rehabilitative Ideal," in William Petersen and David Matza (editors), *Social Controversy*, Belmont, Calif.: Wadsworth, 1963, pp. 119–120.

28. Freeman, *op. cit.*, p. 11.

29. As far as I know, he rarely maintains an overall positive stereotype, discounting, as it were, the specific demerits of members of a category—at least he is not inclined in that direction with respect to officialdom.

30. See Daniel Bell's discussion of organized crime as a Coney Island mirror image of American business practices in "Crime as an American Way of Life," *Antioch Review*, Summer 1953, pp. 131–154.

31. The raising of minimal expectations in juvenile codes will be discussed in Chapter 5.

32. The history of many overseer offices in England and America included an initial phase during which the conception of calling was paramount. In those days, the overseers were wealthy volunteers dedicated to character reform and guided by moral zeal. Since then, however, a new professional self-conception has emerged which implies a fundamentally different posture.

33. The only offices of immediate relevance are judge and clergyman since only they oversee delinquents. The measure in which the others mentioned possess a warrant to preach is relatively unimportant.

34. The preaching of marginal professionals is probably resented irrespective of whether it takes the form of "hard-sell" pontificating or "soft-sell" counseling.

Custom, Tort, and Injustice

Two components of justice remain: commensurability and comparison. Each will be discussed but, first, a short detour must be made. Subcultural viewpoints regarding the comparability of the treatment accorded juveniles with other statuses and those regarding the relation between crime and punishment are best understood in a context of more general views regarding the proper realm and scope of criminal law.

The definition of an act as a crime or a delinquency permits the intervention of the state. That is the common element shared by otherwise disparate acts, and that is why a conception of infraction may organize the study of delinquent behavior. Every commission of an act that is defined as criminal is an authorization of official action. That is all we can be sure they have in common. The purpose of authorized interference has traditionally been the protection of the sovereign and the citizenry. In democratic nations, however, the authorization of state intervention in the form of criminal law has been limited and restricted in the interests of maintaining personal and local prerogatives. Such limitations on the state have been at the heart of democratic institutions. Thus, the criminal law is fundamentally a political matter since it has been one major focus of the ongoing conflict between authorized officials of the state and the citizenry.[1]

One major way of framing the ongoing tension between the state and the citizenry has been to conceive of the encroachment of state-enforced prohibitions on the customs of the citizenry. It has long been obvious that the criminal law, in which the state announces in advance when its intervention is authorized, may depart from the customary morals of the citizenry. In criminology such departures have been noted but not always appreciated partly because of the positivist focus on criminal motivations without reference to law. When positivism came to include the subject's attitude to law, it did so in a grand manner which grossly oversimplified the relation between law and custom. It posited an oppositional delinquent subculture. The effect of such a conception has been to obscure the complicated relation between law and public opinion—a relation that combines consent and dissent.

The relation of law to custom has been a central issue in jurisprudence. There, differing views regarding the relation have served to identify differing or conflicting positions on the proper nature of law and its origins and functions. Cohen, Robson, and Bates suggest:

> One of the most recurrent themes in legal literature . . . [has been] . . . the relationship of law to morals. From this common theme have sprung the variations that characterize and distinguish many different approaches to the nature and function of law. John Chapman Gray, for example, . . . "in a case where there is nothing to guide him but the notion of right and wrong" . . . would take note of the moral sentiment of the community, but not feel bound to follow it. Cardoza, on the other hand, would, in such a situation, feel himself "under a duty to conform to the accepted standards of the community, the *mores* of the times." [2]

Despite the fact that varying positions have emerged with respect to the actual and proper relation of law to custom, legal spokesmen have long realized that the relation is inherently a complex one, especially in pluralistic societies like our own. Judge Learned Hand reflects on the intricacy of the relation in commenting on the difficulty of ascertaining the proper moral response to a conflict between law and ethics. His comments were made specifically with reference to a case of mercy killing, but they have more general applicability. What is man to do in the event of a conflict between legal expectations and deeply held customary morals? Judge Hand says:

> Indeed, in the case at the bar itself the answer is not wholly certain; for we all know that there are great numbers of people of the most unimpeachable virtue, who think it is morally justifiable to put an end

to a life so inexorably destined to be a burden to others,—and—so far as any possible interest of its own is concerned—condemned to a brutish existence, lower indeed than all but the lowest forms of sentient life. Nor is it inevitably an answer to say that it must be immoral to do this, until the law provides security against the abuses that would inevitably follow, unless the practice were regulated. Many people— probably most people—do not make it a final ethical test of conduct that it shall not violate law; few of us exact of ourselves or of others the unflinching obedience of a Socrates. There being no lawful means of accomplishing an end, which they believe to be righteous in itself, there have always been conscientious persons who feel no scruple in acting in defiance of a law which is repugnant to their personal convictions, and who even regard as martyrs those who suffer by doing so. In our own history it is only necessary to recall the abolitionists.[3]

Thus, executives of law themselves recognize the occasional tendency for ethical demands to override legal expectations. This tendency may manifest itself in a variety of ways and in different segments of the population. Though generally we associate such principled behavior with persons possessing strong moral convictions, conflicts between ethical demands and law may arise in groups which in the main seem rather immoral. Ethical demands may override legal expectations in the companies of subcultural delinquency. The expectations implicit in criminal law may be neutralized by ethical canons implicit in common childhood customs which attain a special prominence among subcultural delinquents.

Virtue, Mitigation, and Commensurability

Few of us would have trouble in joining Judge Hand in his retrospective indulgence of the illegal behavior of the abolitionists. Their actions were not only inspired by moral conviction, they subsequently became lawful; just as George Washington's many traitorous acts were happily converted to patriotism. In the realm of political crime, we have come to appreciate the occasional conflict between ethical principles and law. Moreover, the relativity of virtuous patriotism and unlawful treason is patent. One need not succumb to rampant relativism—the frivolous view that law is completely arbitrary—to appreciate the fact that in juvenile crime, too, the offender *occasionally* sees his offense as prompted by virtue and justifies it accordingly. The virtues that prompt illegal behavior among juveniles are obviously not political in character; instead, they are rather childish. However, these childish virtues are among the most primordial of human ideals, neglected in some societies but almost never wholly forgotten. The virtues I allude to are those stressing the traditional precepts of manliness, celebrating as they do the heroic themes of honor, valor, and loyalty.

Valor and loyalty are among the most traditional of manly virtues. But the fact that something is a manly virtue does not mean that its celebration will necessarily predominate among actual or accomplished men. On the contrary, outlanders—those who look in longingly from the outside—typically outdo actual incumbents in the frenzy and dedication with which they pursue ideals. Outlanders with respect to manhood—youth—are characteristically among the most vehement promulgators of the manly virtues of valor and loyalty. Youth stand at the threshold of manhood, and consequently they are more obsessed by the postures and poses that symbolize and confirm it. Accomplished men need considerably less confirmation, and are for a variety of reasons gradually converted to the ideals of prudence, realism, and compromise which make up an important component of what we commonly mean by maturity.

As compared to other youth, the adherents of subcultural delinquency are especially entranced by the time-honored precepts of manliness. Manliness is their special anxiety and obsession, reflected and aggravated, as suggested earlier, by the form, content, and frequency of their most common activity—sounding. Thus, the general concern of youth with the symbolic confirmation of manhood is somewhat magnified among subcultural delinquents. In their barbed repartée, flamboyant defiance, recklessness, and their adherence to the virtues of valor and loyalty, they come close to exemplifying precocious manhood.

The defense and maintenance of reputation are familiar motives of action. Subcultural delinquents reveal their concern with maintaining a reputation for valor by frequent reiteration and reference to key terms in their vocabulary. Terms like "rep" and "heart" pertain directly to the issue of valor as does the derogatory

appellation "chicken." These terms—or more up-to-date equivalents—are central in the delinquent jargon. Delinquent terminol-
ogy, and presumably the priority of motives it reflects, pays special attention to the conspicuous display of manly courage. Insults
are not to be regarded lightly. Though they may be verbally
ployed instead of physically countered, they must be met. The
option of violent counteraction to insult is available even though
it may not always be utilized. Dares and challenges—forms of
anticipatory insult—must be handled without undue loss of face
or reputation despite the fact that they may be and are evaded.
It is not that one must inevitably succumb to challenge and dare
or avenge every insult; instead, one must merely be alert to the
ways in which they may be gracefully evaded, occasionally confronted, and, in any event, reacted to in manly fashion.

Dare, challenge, and insult are most likely to occur in the public situation of company. The subcultural delinquent in that situation is "on," in that he is under pressure to persuasively perform.[4]
Unfortunately, he has taken upon himself the hazardous enterprise of performing a part in which he is obviously miscast. He
wishes to demonstrate that he is a man. He is not, and thus he is
driven to extravagant and incredible bravado.

The stress on valor is usually connected with a high evaluation
of loyalty. Both are among the traditional martial virtues.[5] They
are bound together by a conception of reputation. Reputation reveals a concern with how one appears before others, and the
urgency of maintaining it depends on the depth of belief in group
solidarity. Thus, valor is most assiduously pursued in groups that
celebrate the precepts of loyalty. However, the celebration of
group solidarity and loyalty may not reflect actual group relations. Unstable and shaky groups may come to stress loyalty and
solidarity and thus mask the brittle bonds that tie it together.
Just as outlandish youth may become the prime exponents of the
virtues of manliness, conflict-ridden companies may develop harsh
and totalitarian expectations of loyalty. The demand for total
loyalty is made not because it has been or can be gained but, instead, because the company has become so discontentedly accustomed to losing membership.

Loyalty is a basic issue in the subculture of delinquency partially because its adherents are so regularly disloyal. They regu-

larly abandon the company at the age of remission for more conventional pursuits. However, there is another reason for the fear of disloyalty and consequent obsession with the testing of loyalty. Delinquent companies, after all, are involved in illegal enterprise. Sanctionable behavior is common knowledge. Every act of defection introduces the threat of exposure and apprehension. Consequently, loyalty must be regularly certified. Total loyalty is exhibited by the commission of risky and dangerous acts for purposes of reputation. Certification may be accomplished by periodic checks of just how far a member will go in currying the favor of peers and the leaders who speak for them. Challenges and dares may be used to test the reputation of the member, and simultaneously to check on the credibility of his membership.

Thus, valor and loyalty achieve the status of customary morals in the subculture of delinquency. Like many of the lofty ethical sentiments appearing in the conventional world, they are commonly honored in the breach. But they are celebrated nonetheless, and pursued in characteristically childish fashion. Whenever such customary morals are strongly entrenched, they may occasionally conflict with legal expectations. When they do, as in the case of boys who "just went along" on a joy ride in a stolen car because they did not wish to "leave their buddies flat," or did not wish to appear "chicken," we may suspect that in the eyes of the offender the offense is at least partially mitigated by his virtuous motive. It is not, as a theory of a delinquent subculture would imply, that the stealing of a car is esteemed and demanded behavior; rather, that going along with one's buddies and not chickening out are in the nature of boyish ethics. Accordingly, subcultural delinquents do not typically believe the offense to be negated by the circumstance of a conflicting customary conviction. They merely hold the offense to be mitigated. The act is still wrong, and warrants official intervention; but *less wrong* because it was motivated and inspired by sentiments that in a different context everybody would consider fine and noble. Thus, the illegal behavior obscures an ethical act, and unless the virtuous motive is brought to light and appreciated through a mitigation of the penalty, the subcultural delinquent comes to feel that common standards of justice are violated. And, in a coarse and childish way, he is partially right. We normally encourage—through mass media and more informal channels—youth to believe that valor and loyalty are virtuous. Moreover, it is part of the common sense that evil behavior which is prompted wholly or partially by noble motive is in that measure transformed and thus warrants special consideration and mitigation of penalty.

When the law precludes customary virtues like valor and loyalty from the restricted list of circumstances that may properly mitigate *mens rea*, it provides yet another occasion for the sensing of injustice.[6] When no consideration is given the virtuous motivation of an infraction, the expectation of commensurability is violated. Commensurability refers to the relation between infraction and sanction. What you do to me should in some measure be related to what I have done. Moreover, the phrase "what I have done" must be understood in context and full complexity. It will not do, from the viewpoint of the accused—it probably never has—for justice to blind itself to the possibly human or noble motives that inspired an evil act. But blind itself, at least partially, is precisely what justice must do if it is to avoid the temptation of continuously enlarging the circumstances mitigating *mens rea*. There is perhaps an inescapable difference of perspective between those who judge and those undergoing judgment, the former pressing for the limitation of legitimate consideration of the context of act, the latter pressing for more complete consideration. Those who judge can never completely understand, for if they could they would in that measure no longer be able to render routine judgment.

When acts commonly assumed evil are prompted by ethical considerations, the nature of the offense may be transformed. The offense is mitigated according to the tenets of subcultural delinquency. From the perspective of legal officials, the offense ordinarily remains unmitigated. Occasionally the offense may be aggravated since it has been inspired by so unreasonable a motive as maintaining a "rep" or "going along with the rest of the fellas." These motives may appear unreasonable because they may impress officials with the grave extent to which the accused is immersed in delinquency.[7] Such cases may occasionally elicit harsher sanction or disapproval than might otherwise have occurred. Subcultural delinquents, in response, sense injustice because instituted authority has remained oblivious to the issue of commensurability, and feigned ignorance of traditional extralegal sources of mitigation. Moreover, the virtuous motives of infraction are not the only element of custom ignored by officials. There is another aspect of custom that demands consideration if justice taken as commensurability is to be done.

Consensual Crime and Prohibition

There is virtual consensus in modern society on the sanctionable nature of many acts that violate the criminal law. Offenses committed against the person or those against property make up the core of substantive criminal law. Virtually no one, not even subcultural delinquents, would care to dissent from the common belief that offenses of that variety warrant the intervention of state authority. However, such infractions do not exhaust the substance of criminal law. There are other acts that law regards as sanctionable, some of which fail to gain the popular legitimacy accorded offenses against person and property.

Segments of public opinion and law may conflict on the wisdom or necessity of interfering with some forms of conduct. Consequently, law may appear unjust even when it manifests concern with commensurability, as it does by typically reserving its harshest sanctions for consensual crimes and applying lesser sanctions for those that fail to gain overwhelming popular consent. It appears unjust because it has failed to be *sufficiently* concerned with commensurability. The penalty for gambling or illicit use of alcohol or marihuana may be light but, for some members of society, not light enough. For many offenses lying at the periphery of criminal law—typically offenses in which no victim is apparent—there is a segment of the population that is more or less given to abolitionist sentiment. Their opinion of many prohibited acts is that, while perhaps lacking virtue or utility, they are not sufficiently evil or harmful to warrant state concern and suppression. According to an abolitionist view, the state, by concerning itself with such petty matters, violates the rights of citizens to engage in minor failings, and, moreover, displays an insensitivity to commensurability—the relation between the gravity of infraction and the reaction to it.

The institution of consensual crimes requires little continuous justification. Such crimes are socially defined by the citizenry as well as the sovereign as self-evidently wrong and harmful. Such infractions as murder, robbery, assault, burglary, rape, and others are ordinarily conceived to be so self-evidently wrong that the citizenry considers them *mala in se*. They are bad in themselves, and the matter rarely receives any further discussion. Other acts, however, are not so self-evidently wrong. They do not so obviously warrant the intervention of the state, and thus their prohibition is a topic of debate and discussion both among experts and the ordinary citizenry. These acts are in effect *mala prohibita*. They are "things in themselves indifferent" but prohibited or tolerated "as the municipal legislator sees proper, for promoting the welfare of the society, and more effectively carrying on the purposes of civil life." [8] When acts are considered themselves indifferent—when, in other words, the wisdom of suppressing them is debatable—we may refer to such acts as "prohibitions" if they are written into the criminal law. They are nonetheless crimes because they elicit authorized state intervention, but they are different from other crimes in failing to self-evidently warrant intervention. Crimes that self-evidently warrant state intervention may be referred to as "consensual crimes."

Whenever segments of the community remain unimpressed with the legitimacy of a specific prohibition, a heavy burden rests on the authority of the state. The officials of state authority are burdened because they cannot depend as much on voluntary abstinence, and have little access to a community of ready complainants and witnesses in the enforcement of the prohibition. Moreover, the state is burdened by the taint of injustice. The abolitionist segment of the community which either vocally opposes, or in deed flaunts the prohibition, is likely to be struck by the oppressive and overbearing character of state authority. The state, as frequently occurs, comes to be viewed as a busybody, poking its nose into the private affairs of the citizenry. Its intervention, however light the sanction in the event of apprehension, is taken as a violation of commensurability and thus justice.

Subcultural delinquents hold implicit views on the legitimacy of a variety of offenses. Offenses against the person and property, as suggested, are held to be self-evidently wrong and warrant state intervention. In other offenses, however, the subcultural delinquent tacitly takes what amounts to an abolitionist position. In sentiment and deed, he holds many acts to be indifferent in themselves and dissents from the propriety of prohibiting them. There are two major kinds of prohibitions that elicit an abolitionist response from the subculture of delinquency. In both varieties of prohibition—vices and status prohibitions—the subcultural delinquent senses a violation of justice. The prohibition of vices raises the issue of commensurability; status prohibitions that of comparability.

Vice and Commensurability

The customary belief that certain admittedly unrighteous acts do not warrant official prohibition is a special and limiting case of the concern with commensurability. The abolitionist position suggests that the proper state reaction to vice is tolerance or indifference. Anything more is incommensurable with the gravity of the failing.

Divided public opinion regarding the propriety of prohibiting vice is one of the most important examples of the conflict between law and custom. A key distinction between abolitionist and prohibitionist sentiment pertains to differing attitudes regarding the proper relation between law and customary morals. The abolitionist leans to the view that law should reflect customary morals, whereas the prohibitionist tends to believe that law should serve as an edifying and vanguard institution.[9] However, the distinction between the two can be overdrawn, especially as it appears among legal theorists. Cohen, Robson, and Bates suggest that too great a stress on the conflicting opinions of legal theorists may obscure important elements of consensus. Virtually no legal theorist, and probably very few citizens, are so strongly prohibitionist as to assume the irrelevance of customary morals. As often happens, the full spectrum between opposing viewpoints is hardly used. Consequently, the differences between the abolitionist and prohibitionist positions usually pertain to the measure in which law should be guided by customary morals. "All [legal theorists] would utilize the moral ingredient either as a norm to *consider* or a norm to *follow*." [10] (My stress.) Thus, in democratic societies there has usually been an approximation of consensus on the view that law in some sense ought to reflect community standards. The differences of opinion reappear, however, and are manifested in differing assessments of prevalent community standards and differing judgments of their precise social whereabouts.

The transfer of disagreement to the concrete, factual level and the assumption of consensus on the moral view that law ought in some measure reflect community standards may be illustrated in the dispute between Judges Parker and Hand at an American Law Institute deliberation on a Model Penal Code. Both judges assumed and agreed on the relevance of customary morality in the framing of a model code. However, they disagreed sharply on the temper of prevalent community standards.

Cohen, Robson, and Bates summarize the exchange:

The issue of whether sodomy should be enjoined by law was debated by Judge Parker and Judge Learned Hand. Judge Parker urged that private homosexuality should be prohibited by law because such conduct flies "in the face of public opinion as evidenced by the code of every state of the union." Judge Hand supported the opposite view on the ground that "criminal law which is not enforced practically is much worse than if it was not on the books at all," and that sodomy "is a matter very largely of taste, and is not a matter that people should be put in prison about." [11]

The issue is well stated in the dispute between Judges Parker and Hand. Besides suggesting the agreement between the two on the relevance of customary morality for law, their exchange captures in a nutshell some of the major differences between prohibitionist and abolitionist sentiment. Moreover, their dispute reminds us that differences of viewpoint are not limited to diversely inclined citizens. Differences of opinion appear also within the legal system itself. As both cause and effect of such differences of opinion, the status of prohibitions has been persistently shaky. This shakiness is sometimes manifested in indecisive enforcement and evasive explanation in response to challenge and question. It may be illustrated by an exchange between a police officer and a juvenile who was picked up for drunkenness.[12] The arrested juvenile was in hostile and rebellious spirits and proceeded to challenge the police officer on the justice of arresting someone for merely being drunk. He claimed that it was unfair that juveniles be punished for something adults can do. The police officer appeared nonplussed. Consequently, perhaps, he omitted reminding the juvenile that while he was correct in implying that there are juvenile status offenses—acts which adults may commit with impunity—his particular offense was not among them. Public exhibitions of drunkenness are prohibited for adults as well as juveniles. Instead of speaking to that issue and defending the prohibitionist position, he tacitly took what seemed an abolitionist position modified only by the eternal plea of the functionary. He told the juvenile that perhaps he was right, that maybe drunkenness should not be against the law, but that as things stood, it was. He continued to say that he was just doing his duty as a police officer. It was not for him to decide whether a particular prohibition was warranted or not. The policeman would not debate the principle. He would not support the prohibitionist position despite the fact that the theory and practice of his office committed him to it.

This incident is not recounted to illustrate police malpractice. It may well have been proper practice. I have included it only to suggest that highly visible vacillation and indecision occur in the enforcement of prohibitions, and they do not go unnoticed by subcultural delinquents. The subculture of delinquency takes note and is reinforced by the observation that officials and citizens partially join them in resenting what many police call "chicken shit" offenses.

It is difficult to know with anything approaching certainty which specific prohibitions fail to gain legitimacy among subcultural delinquents. Moreover, it is doubtful that consensus on these matters prevails even in as limited a world as that of subcultural delinquency. For some offenses, like homosexuality or other sexual perversions, there is doubtless a division of opinion among delinquents themselves, some holding to an abolitionist view, others to an indignantly prohibitionist position. For other offenses, like gambling, drinking, or fornication, an overwhelmingly abolitionist view is much more likely. However, subcultural delinquents probably do not hold an abolitionist view regarding these prohibited vices with any great measure of vehemence because that perceived injustice is obscured by another which is more specifically directed to them. They are not so struck by the incommensurable penalty attending the commission of vice because they are partially distracted by a different and more immediate prohibition, one which subsumes the vices but is not limited to them.

Status Prohibitions and Comparison

Justice in its comparative component consists of a concern with the reasoned and tenable quality of the noticeably different expectations which sometimes apply to different statuses. The juvenile status is perhaps the most important specially treated status remaining in American life.[13] Youth is among the few surviving categories in American life that in principle as well as practice remains outside the blanket of legal equality.

Status prohibitions are an important aspect of the special legal position of juveniles in America. This special penalty of youth is in some measure balanced by special indulgences in the form of light sentencing, more frequent use of probation than in adult cases, and other judicial niceties. Whether the special indulgence matches the special penalty is an interesting issue to debate, but such speculation is almost surely idle. Whatever the considered conclusions of objective or disinterested observers, it would be foolish to expect subcultural delinquents, given their interested perspective and position, to be impressed with the ways in which their special liability is matched by favored treatment. Like most members of society, especially dependents, they are more likely to be impressed with the special liabilities of their status than its privileges.[14]

A traditional justification for instituting prohibitions has been the protection and enhancing of community welfare and morality. Thus, it was perhaps to be expected that dependent statuses would be subjected frequently to special prohibitions inapplicable to more complete participants in civic life. Dependent statuses are populated by persons who have been ascribed neither full citizenship nor maturity. Thus, they have seemed fitting subjects of special prohibitions. Special prohibitions have been seen as a basic part of their special protection.[15]

Justifications for prohibitions applicable only to youth have abounded. They have included a desire to protect the innocent from temptation, and a related suspiciousness regarding the unrestrained propensities of "hot-blooded" youth.[16] More recently, special prohibitions have been justified, especially by exponents of enlightened treatment methods, by reference to their preventive and diagnostic function. If runaway is predictive of other more serious offenses, and if during a runaway one frequently steals, are we not wiser to prohibit runaway too, and thus happily enable the authorities to intervene earlier and more easily in misdirected lives? The question is an old one. The only thing new is that currently the question is incomprehensibly put rhetorically, as if the advisability and wisdom of preventive justice were self-evident.

The reaction of youth to status prohibitions is mixed. Some youth apparently concur in the legitimacy of such prohibitions, others dissent, and many are uncertain and vacillating. Subcultural delinquents apparently object, sometimes quite vociferously, to the special demands incumbent upon them and other minors.

The sense in which juveniles are subjected to special demands is simple and consequential. Juvenile codes in the United States add a great assortment of prohibitions—applicable only to juveniles—to the ordinary crimes and prohibitions applicable to the whole citizenry.[17] Sol Rubin succinctly summarizes this aspect of the legal status of juveniles. He says:

In the juvenile court acts . . . every definition of delinquency includes violations of [universally applicable] laws and ordinances by children. The definition of delinquency does not, however, stop there, but *starts* there. The list of other acts or conditions which may bring a child within the jurisdiction of the juvenile courts is painstakingly long.[18]

The behavior subsumed by status prohibitions varies from state to state, as does the number of special clauses in the juvenile code. Despite this variation, some similarities emerge. Among the most common status prohibitions are those dealing with habitual truancy, incorrigibility, being beyond the control of parent or guardian, and absenting oneself from home without consent (runaway). Additionally, a variety of acts which are commonplace and permissible for adults are prohibited. These include staying out late, drinking, sexual activity, the driving of cars, and in a few jurisdictions such acts as smoking and swearing. In short, the freedom of choice, action, and movement is much more restricted for juveniles than for adults. For juveniles, criminal law moves significantly in the direction of a statement of maximal rather than minimal social expectations. The fact that such prohibitions are only occasionally enforced is little reason for solace. Sporadic enforcement frequently implies uneven or selective enforcement at the expense of those who are suspected of more serious infractions. Thus, both the existence of such statutes and the fact that they are only occasionally enforced may contribute to the delinquent's sense of injustice. The existence of the prohibition may violate the expectations of comparability, whereas its sporadic enforcement does violence to the even more widespread expectation of consistency.

Adherents of the subculture of delinquency resent the restrictions inherent in status prohibitions. They resent these restrictions because they pertain to activity that comes very close to being the behavioral core of their subculture. In many respects, "messing around," which is one way of rendering the activity enjoined in many status prohibitions, more exemplifies the behavioral substance of the subculture of delinquency than more serious criminal ventures. Getting drunk, acting recklessly, disturbing the peace, annoying and exploiting girls, and, in general, being beyond the control of one's parents and other adults exemplifies the subcultural delinquent. These are the staple activities that make up considerably more of the delinquent round than the behavior forbidden by consensual crimes. The occasion and opportunity for such wild or ungovernable behavior is frequently provided by the freedom from institutional controls implicit in truancy and runaway. Each releases the juvenile from major social control agencies—school and family—and each in a symbolic way converts the juvenile to a precocious adult.

None of the subcultural delinquent's activities better reveal the aim of his enterprise than the daily round that violates the juvenile status prohibitions. In truancy and runaway, both of which temporarily liquidate the institutional foundations of childhood, and in the smoking, drinking, sex- and car-play, all of which substantively violate the hierarchical division of perquisites between juveniles and adults, the subcultural delinquent cues the goals of his enterprise. The assignment of goals to enterprises is always risky, but is perhaps permissible if done only metaphorically and half seriously. So viewed, the goal of subcultural delinquency may be suggested. It is a customary system that incidentally permits and encourages criminal acts, but essentially pursues the gratification deriving from the license of precocious manhood.

Being adult—not through aspiration but through contemporary acts of manly prowess—is a prime concern of subcultural delinquents. Sounding and bravado both reflect and exacerbate the anxious urgency of attaining manhood. Moreover, they reflect and encourage forays into the behavioral world of grownups. Status prohibitions, though they are only rarely stressed in discussions of juvenile delinquency, are central to its understanding since they enlighten a basic antagonism between law and a segment of youth.

The wish to invidiously exhibit manhood is well illustrated by considering the shifting symbolic implications of smoking. Until recently, smoking was a sign of adulthood and, until the feminine emancipation, a perquisite of manhood. Thus, it was an excellent symbol of precocious manhood and, as such, a favorite pastime of subcultural delinquents. Juveniles who smoked, especially if they publicly flaunted their vice, could more or less be assumed to be juvenile delinquents. As customary restrictions on juvenile behavior loosened—as youth, too, gained a measure of emancipation—smoking could no longer suffice in symbolizing the precocious ascent to adulthood. Precociously manly youth were in that respect not terribly different from conventionally childish youth. Many in both categories smoked. Consequently, as is typical among those pursuing illusory symbols, the ante was raised. The invidious display of manhood could no longer be accomplished by ordinary smoking. But it could be symbolized by a more risky form of smoking, a form that could recapture the sense of risk, danger, bravado, and thus manhood implicit in the older definitions of childhood smoking. One may no longer "show off" his precocious manhood by ordinary smoking, but one may do so by extraordinary smoking. Marihuana use among subcultural delinquents may perhaps be best viewed as extraordinary smoking.

An aim and function of status prohibitions is to curtail the possibilities of precocious manhood and the license implicit in such a status. An aim and function of subcultural delinquency is to enhance the possibility and enlarge the scope of precocious manhood. Thus, a basic antagonism exists, but not, it should be reiterated, at the core of the criminal law. The substantive antagonism exists at the frequently neglected periphery of juvenile law. Subcultural delinquents are sensitive to the issue of differential treatment of diverse statuses not because they are generally exponents of the norms of equal treatment; rather because the specific nature of incomparability strikes at the very heart of their airs, poses, and ambitions. By prohibiting truancy and runaway the law has made the unregulated area in which precocious manhood may flourish off-bounds. By prohibiting many forms of specific licentious activities and permitting these same activities for adults, the law has made clear its opinion of what is even to themselves the only defensible aspiration of subcultural delinquents. The law seems to thwart the aspirations of subcultural delinquency and for that it receives incessant hostility and scorn.

Thus far in this chapter, the legitimacy of state intervention has been discussed. I have suggested that in the case of status prohibitions, vice, and consensual crimes prompted by virtuous motives, segments of the population withhold the legitimacy normally granted the elements of criminal law. Such a tacitly abolitionist position is a clear and gross repudiation of specific components of law. It represents a dissent at the material or substantive level of law and, as suggested, is limited to the periphery of criminal law. Now we may return to the more characteristic subcultural dissent that occurs beneath the substantive level. We turn to what may be termed the *methodological* element of law.

Crime and Tort

Law exploits a variety of methods in the maintenance of order. Rights may be vindicated and wrongs suppressed or otherwise discouraged in a variety of ways. Each mode maintains order and community standards of morality by use of a somewhat different method. The final way in which the criminal law is neutralized consists of a methodological dissent in which subcultural delinquents unconsciously elaborate a vulgar conception of tort. They unwittingly assert that under certain conditions the private and compensatory methods of civil law warrant precedence over the public and penal methods of criminal law. In so arguing, they characteristically extend and distort common legal and lay views regarding the proper province of the law of crime and that of tort.

The distinction between crime and tort is not without ambiguity. A great many acts that are sanctionable as crimes are simultaneously torts.[19] Instead of being a source of confusion, however, the considerable substantive overlap between acts that are torts and those that are crimes informs of the essential nature of the distinction. The distinction between tort and crime is not substantive but formal. It consists of a different legal method of vindicating the wrong intrinsic in an act that is socially defined as harmful. The terms tort and crime, when juxtaposed, do not distinguish between different acts but between different legal ways of responding to acts considered harmfully wrong.

Criminal and tort action are among the major legal methods by which remedial actions are obtained.[20] Each mode of remedial action highlights characteristic methods, despite the fact that the differentiation is not complete. Though compensation for harm is the paramount and characteristic function of tort action, it may also on occasion infringe upon the traditional prerogatives of criminal law and be punitive in character. This invasion of the punitive ideas characteristic of criminal law is typically regarded as anomalous and takes the form of "punitive" or "exemplary" damages. Such damages are sometimes awarded "where the defendant's wrongdoing has been intentional and deliberate and has the characteristic of outrage frequently associated with crime."[21] These occasional exceptions aside, the ideas of punishment or of deterrence do not properly play a role in tort actions.

The essential remedial method of tort action is redress or compensation for harm. Other remedial methods are used in tort actions, like injunction, "but the availability of . . . such remedies will depend in the first instance upon the possibility that an action for damages would lie for the wrong thus averted."[22] Thus, a tort is a wrong, other than breach of contract (the latter falls under the law of contracts which covers specific agreements and promises) in which the legal remedy consists of damages paid to a righteous plaintiff.

The remedial method of the criminal law is considerably different. The method of criminal law is penal sanction. This, as I have stressed throughout, is the signature of criminal law irrespective of whether the sanction is aimed at retaliation or rehabilitation, irrespective of whether the sentence is meted out, postponed as in probation, mercifully put aside as in suspension, or prematurely culminated as in parole. Fines, too, which along with imprisonment and death currently exhaust the method of penal sanction, differ fundamentally from the payment of damages in civil action. Fines are paid to the state and not to a plaintiff—and for good and fundamental reason. A crime is not committed against an individual; it is committed against the public at large. This statement cannot be treated as a mere fiction. It is central to an understanding of the remedial method of criminal law, and subsequently to an appreciation of the subcultural delinquent's dissent from legal precepts.[23]

The differences between criminal and other kinds of law are based on the serious assertion that a crime is an offense against the public at large. A major purpose of criminal law is to intercede between the accused and the victim, and to literally transform the act into one in which the state, acting as representative of the public, becomes the victim and thus the plaintiff. The factual victim, the individual who was the object of the harmful wrong, recedes in importance. In a sense, the victim's role is even more transformed in the shift from tort to crime than that of the accused. Not only is a criminal action completely oblivious to the idea of compensating the injured or otherwise victimized individual; his part in the proceeding is drastically cut. He is "an accuser and a witness for the state."[24] Except insofar as the state depends on the victim for testimony, he loses all of the prerogatives that are his in civil action. As we shall see, the prerogatives of the victim and, more generally, his central role in the proceeding are restored in the viewpoint of subcultural delinquency.

In American criminal law, the injured person is relegated to a minor role in proceedings against the accused. This is a fundamental difference between criminal and tort law. A tort action "is commenced and maintained by the injured person himself, and its purpose is to compensate him for the damage he has suffered at the expense of the wrongdoer. If he is successful he receives a judgment for a sum of money, which he may enforce by collecting it from the defendant." [25] Tort actions vindicate personal rights. The purpose of criminal proceedings is different. The aim of criminal proceedings is to "vindicate the interests of the public as a whole, by punishing the offender or eliminating him from society, either permanently or for a limited time, by reforming him or teaching him not to repeat the offense, and by deterring others from imitating him." [26]

Though the considerable substantive overlap between torts and crimes may be exploited in eliminating epiphenomenal and locating essential differences, the same overlap obviously introduces a fundamental and persistent ambiguity. To distinguish tort and crime in terms of legal response rather than the substantive act may be helpful, but it entails a partial begging of the question. What we may really wish to know when asking about the distinction is precisely what seemed at first to answer the question: when is it that law responds to a harmful wrong as tort and when as a crime? The existence of considerable substantive overlap— the fact that many acts may be legally responded to either as torts, crimes, or both—means that no clear-cut answer is possible. Whether a harmful wrong is legally responded to as tort or crime, or both, seems often to depend on the particular situation rather than general explanatory principles. Thus, an important element of ambiguity remains and is unavoidable in the distinction between crime and tort. Characteristically, dissenting subcultural views develop and flourish in areas of legal ambiguity. Characteristically, the differences between subcultural and legal views dwarf the differences that appear within the legal system itself.

Prerogatives of the Victim

A key element in construing a harmful wrong a tort instead of a crime is a narrow focusing on the victim and his prerogatives. To make private, or depublicize, the nature of a harmful act is to tacitly believe that it warrants treatment as a tort instead of a crime. A concern with the victim and his prerogatives may serve to obliterate or obscure from view the public element and thus the criminal nature of the harmful act. If the wrong can be conceived as a private transaction between the accused and the victim, a crucial step has been taken in neutralizing criminal law.

Just such a view pervades the subculture of delinquency. The automatic designation of some harmful wrongs as crimes is interfered with by subcultural conceptions. According to subcultural precept, automatic designation is hardly warranted. Sometimes the state ought to intervene; sometimes not. The initiating of the criminal process ought to be up to the victim. It was, after all, he who was hurt.

Subcultural delinquents frequently believe that the criminal process cannot be invoked unless the victim is willing to press the charge or make a complaint. They are substantially right, but for the wrong reason. Their error is initially rooted in a common childish equivocation, perhaps the most common of all equivocations. Their equivocation is based on the confusion or equation of the *factual* and *moral* imperatives inherent in the term "can" and its negative "cannot." The subcultural view stressing the prerogatives of the victim builds on this initially equivocal use of imperatives.

When the criminal process cannot be invoked because the victim is unwilling to make a complaint, it is because in many cases the victim's participation, as a witness, is absolutely essential. The term "cannot" is obviously used here in its factually imperative sense. However, as every schoolteacher knows, many children use the term "cannot" to refer also to a negative *moral* imperative, and so understand it. They say cannot instead of may not. Consequently, they mistake the meaning of the common allegation that the police cannot press charges unless the complainant wishes them to. They take it to mean that the police may not; and subsequently they come to strengthen the moral imperative and believe that the police ought not intervene unless the victim wishes them to.

Such a confusion is common but rarely so consequential. The initial confusion, and the peculiar views that build on and survive it, amounts to the assertion that tort rather than criminal law ought to reign. It results in a view that grants the victim the same initiative in criminal as in tort action. By personalizing the wrong, the delinquent retrieves the right of automatic intervention granted the state in criminal law. However, the similarity between the delinquent viewpoint and actual tort action ends there. The subcultural delinquent is largely unaware of the legal distinction between crime and tort, and thus he gets the two methods hopelessly confused. The victim's prerogatives are restored but he may exercise them, if desired, through invoking the criminal instead of the civil process. However, he need not. The victim may also forget about the offense, pardon or excuse the accused, or take upon himself the burden of vindication. To invoke the criminal process or not ought to be, according to the subcultural delinquent, up to the victim.

An awarding of a central role to the victim in initiating the criminal process is, for the delinquent, a safeguard against the enforcement of law against petty violations. Who better than the victim can judge whether a wrong involved the infliction of meaningful harm or was, instead, a bit of harmless mischief? Surely, one would not wish to leave this weighty and personal decision to officials who have not experienced the concrete wrong, or on other grounds gained a reputation as dependable or competent. In believing that a substantially felt personal injury is a precondition for invoking the criminal process, subcultural delinquents reveal again the sense in which rudimentary conceptions of tort pervade their mentality. A stress on personal injury privatizes the infraction by allowing the introduction of the subjective feelings of the victim and also, by extension, considerations of the relative deprivation he has suffered. The injury may be meaningful or trivial according to the possessions and qualities of the victim. Consequently, the wrong is not automatically so harmful as to warrant the designation crime. Depending on the subjective qualities of the victim and his readiness to forgive, the infraction may be seen as too trivial to warrant state intervention. When the state intervenes, as it sometimes does—subcultural precepts notwithstanding—the delinquent is likely to sense injustice on grounds of incommensurability. He may sense injustice since state officials have failed to consider the victim's main prerogative—his capacity to personally mitigate or even negate the offense.

The Denial of the Victim

Just as the qualities of the victim may render him the kind of person for whom the wrong is too trivial to invoke the criminal process, so his qualities may be so debased as to disqualify him from that right. The imposition of rudiments of a tort conception on to the criminal law is just the beginning of the delinquent distortion culminating in neutralization. Once the personalizing of wrong implicit in the awarding of a central role to the victim is accomplished, the way is prepared for a further stretching of conceptions.

The intrusion of elements of conventional morality, vulgarized to be sure, is nowhere clearer than in the delinquent's occasional denial of the victim. The persons who are denied the normal prerogatives of the victim are the conventionally immoral and the conventionally detested. Homosexuals and other sexual perverts, drunkards, chiselers, members of debased minorities, or members of discredited political groups may, because of their own failings, forfeit the right to initiate the criminal process. This is best seen in the exploitation of homosexuals common among subcultural delinquents.[27] Here again we may observe the alchemy by which a factual imperative is confused and subsequently converted to a moral imperative. Homosexuals who indulge in relations with delinquents cannot press charges or complain when they are subsequently victimized. They cannot because they would expose themselves to considerable penal sanction. The factual imperative is gradually converted to a moral imperative. They may not or ought not complain since by their own immoral conduct they have forfeited that right. Who are *they* to complain of others? The conversion of crime to tort allows the question of moral competence to be raised in a somewhat peculiar way. Since in the delinquent conception of tort the victim occupies the central initiatory role, he is himself implicated in the process of judgment. Thus, the question of moral competence typically addressed to officials may be extended to victims: who are you to sit in judgment of me?

Whenever the state invokes the criminal process without the permission of the victim, or when it invokes it in behalf of a discredited and thus denied victim, it violates the traditional precepts of subcultural delinquency. It leaves itself open to the charge of injustice on the grounds of incommensurability. Depending on the particular situation, its action may be incommensurable in the sense that sheer intervention may be seen by delinquents as unwarranted, or it may be incommensurable in the sense of failing to consider the mitigating circumstances implicit in the victim's willingness to forgive or his discredited character.

A sense of injustice pervades the subculture of delinquency. This sense is based on its perspective of the official system, and on its curious conceptions of custom and tort. The role played by the sense of injustice is to weaken the bind of law and thus ready the way for the immediate condition of neutralization—the negation of intent. Neutralization enables drift. It is the process by which we are freed from the moral bind of law. As I have stressed throughout, the process of neutralization takes shape and is interwoven with the legal system itself. Subcultural delinquency is an *illegal* system in the strict sense of that term. It is the other side of the legal system. Its precepts and postures are childish responses to official action and childish distortions of lawful precepts. Subcultural delinquency is not a simple ignoring or negation of law; instead, it is complexly related to law and exists in symbiotic antagonism with it. Just as the law comes to be a response to violation, so too the ideology that sponsors violation comes to be a response to law. It is in that sense that delinquency is better viewed as infraction than as action.

Drift is made possible by the neutralization of criminal law and, subsequently, by the temporary liquidation of the bind between the actor and legal order. The points at which neutralization may take place are noteworthy since they indicate, again, the sense in which infraction is an organizing principle of crime and delinquency. *Neutralization consists of obliterating the infractious nature of behavior. It converts infraction to mere action.* This is accomplished by subcultural dissent from principles that constitute the *foundations* of the criminal law. Criminal law is founded not so much on the substantive acts it deems unlawful; rather on principles that define its proper realm and procedure. These principles may be thought of as the conditions under which the intervention, apprehension, and sanction implicit in criminal law are morally permissible. They are, to use an old term, the social contract. The foundations of criminal law appear in the principles and doctrines that concern themselves with the mental, procedural, consensual, and methodological elements. Consequently, it is at these points that the criminal law may be neutralized; and all the easier and more likely when precepts and practices prevalent within the legal machinery themselves lend credence and subterranean support to the dissenting beliefs of subcultural delinquency.

NOTES

1. This point is usually ignored, especially by spokesmen for the juvenile court and other forms of enlightened justice. Such spokesmen and their criminological and psychiatric entourage often assume the posture of vanguard liberals. However, they reveal their essential conservatism by the telltale assumptions of the benevolence of the state and the harmony of interest between state and citizenry. By alluding to these essentially conservative assumptions, I do not intend any facile classification of the complicated and mysterious ideology of the modern treatment viewpoint. I mention them only because liberals are often asked—in the name of liberalism—to refrain from serious criticism of the juvenile court and the treatment viewpoint because, it is alleged, the reactionaries will pounce on such critiques and use them for their own malevolent purposes. My feeling is that it has been a rather remarkable error to confuse these recent juridical innovations with liberalism. They may be good or bad, effective or ineffective, but they are not in the tradition of political liberalism. For a more traditional liberal view stressing the political nature of criminal law and the conflict between state and citizenry, see Francis A. Allen, "Criminal Justice, Legal Values and the Rehabilitative Ideal," *Journal of Criminal Law, Criminology and Police Science,* September–October 1959, and "The Borderland of the Criminal Law," *Social Service Review,* June 1958.
2. J. Cohen, R. A. H. Robson, and A. Bates, "Ascertaining the Moral Sense of the Community," *Journal of Legal Education,* Vol. VIII, No. 2, 1955, p. 137.
3. *Repouille v. United States,* in Richard C. Donnelly, Joseph Goldstein, and Richard D. Schwartz, *Criminal Law,* New York: Free Press of Glencoe, 1962, p. 125.
4. Sheldon Messinger, Harold Sampson, and Robert Towne, "Life as Theatre," *Sociometry,* March 1962.
5. Carl Stephenson, *Medieval Feudalism,* Ithaca, N. Y.: Great Seal, 1956, pp. 51–52; Joseph Margolis, "Juvenile Delinquents: Latter-Day Knights," *The American Scholar,* Spring 1960.
6. This, despite the fact that I and most others would probably concur in the wisdom of rigidly restricting the list of circumstances that legitimately mitigate intent. We cannot always expect things that seem prudent and wise to have wholly happy consequences.

7. For a discussion of the special concern of officials with culturally supported crime, see Richard Cloward and Lloyd Ohlin, *Delinquency and Opportunity*, Glencoe, Ill.: Free Press, 1960, Chap. 1.

8. Thus, my distinction between consensual crimes and prohibitions is not too different from the old distinction between *mala in se* and *mala prohibita*. The only difference is that I obviously do not intend to imply that acts are *in themselves* one or the other. Instead, they are socially defined in a somewhat culturally variable way as one or the other by ordinary members of society. For a summary and elaboration of Blackstone's classic rendition of the distinction between *mala in se* and *prohibita*, see Jerome Hall, *Principles of Criminal Law*, Indianapolis: Bobbs-Merrill, 1960, pp. 337–338. Hall surmises that the distinction is not terribly useful for purposes of jurisprudential or sociological analysis. One could hardly disagree. However, despite its faults, the distinction has more or less survived in the common sense. It is a social distinction implicitly made by subcultural delinquents and many other members of society. Thus, it requires attention. It should not be adopted by sociologists; rather, it should be considered as one element in the citizenry's customary reaction to law.

9. Needless to say, one need not be consistently abolitionist or prohibitionist. We may vary according to the specific matter at hand. Thus, many liberals today are abolitionist with regard to homosexuality and prohibitionist with regard to bigotry.

10. Cohen, Robson, and Bates, *op. cit.*, p. 138.

11. *Ibid.*, p. 139.

12. This is an incident that occurred while I was observing arrest and interrogation procedures.

13. For a detailed summary of the special legal status of juveniles, see Grace Abbott, *The Child and the State*, Chicago: University of Chicago Press, 1938.

14. For a fuller discussion of youth as a dependent status, see my "Patterns of Youth," in Robert Faris (editor), *Handbook of Sociology*, New York: Rand-McNally, forthcoming.

15. T. H. Marshall, *Citizenship and Social Class, and Other Essays*, Cambridge, Eng.: University Press, 1950.

16. For a discussion of the stereotype of hot-blooded youth, see Edgar Friedenberg, "The Image of the Adolescent Minority," *Dissent*, Spring 1963.

17. For a summary of juvenile codes in the United States, see Frederick Sussman, *Laws of Juvenile Delinquency*, New York: Oceana, 1959.

18. Sol Rubin, *Crime and Juvenile Delinquency*, New York: Oceana, 1961, p. 49. The only qualification necessary in Rubin's statement regarding the definition of delinquency is to exclude from it jurisdictions that have no definition of delinquency at all. There are, according to Paul Tappan, eight very, very enlightened juvenile court jurisdictions "where delinquency is not defined at all in their statutes but only the jurisdictional powers of the court." For a penetrating discussion of this and other

features of juvenile justice, see *Comparative Survey of Juvenile Delinquency, Part I: North America,* New York: United Nations, Department of Economic and Social Affairs, 1958, p. 2.

19. For an interesting discussion of the extensive substantive overlap between tort and criminal statutes, see Clarence Morris, *Studies in the Law of Tort,* Brooklyn: Foundation Press, 1952, Chap. 4.

20. Here and below, I follow the concise and useful summary statements on tort by William L. Prosser, *Handbook on the Law of Torts,* St. Paul, Minn.: West, 1955, pp. 1–8; and Warren A. Seavey, "Principles of Torts," *Harvard Law Review,* September 1942, pp. 72–98.

21. Prosser, *op. cit.,* p. 8.

22. Prosser, *op. cit.,* pp. 1–2.

23. It is a humorous irony that the subcultural delinquent tendency to frequently favor a tort rather than a criminal construction of his misdeeds is given lip service, but no more, by the spokesmen of enlightened justice. The juvenile court, they like to say, is a civil court.

24. Prosser, *op. cit.,* p. 7.

25. *Ibid.*

26. *Ibid.*

27. Albert J. Reiss, "The Social Integration of Queers and Peers," *Social Problems,* Fall 1961, pp. 102–120.

[6]

Drifting into Delinquency

THE periodic breaking of the moral bind to law arising from neutralization and resulting in drift does not assure the commission of a delinquent act. Drift makes delinquency possible or permissible by temporarily removing the restraints that ordinarily control members of society, but of itself it supplies no irreversible commitment or compulsion that would suffice to thrust the person into the act. The search for such an impetus, and a veritable insistence on a specification of it, has been largely responsible for the premature dismissal of social control theories. Cohen and Short exemplify the general dissatisfaction with such theories. They suggest that "It is a defect of many of our theories of delinquency that they try to account for delinquency by demonstrating the absence of effective restraints." [1] Social control theories are incomplete or in error because, according to the same writers, "Delinquency . . . cannot be assumed to be a potentiality of human nature which automatically erupts when the lid is off." [2] How deal with this objection? Apparently, the moral vacuum implicit in the removal of cultural restraints is not sufficient to explain the occurrence of delinquency. There is a missing element—an element in the nature of a thrust or an impetus—by which the possibility of delinquency is realized. That element, as suggested in the first chapter, has characteristically been construed in positivist criminology as one or another form of compulsion or commitment. I wish to recommend another construction of that element—a construction that is more consistent with the canons of classical criminology. I wish to suggest that the missing element which provides the thrust or impetus by which the delinquent act is realized is *will*.

181

Entering the Infraction

If the realization of the potential for delinquency implicit in drift merely required the commission of a naive act that happened to be defined as delinquent by some distant officials in society, there would be no necessity to posit as unfamiliar a sociological conception as will. We could rely merely on human nature, for Cohen and Short are not unequivocally right when they say "Delinquency . . . cannot be assumed to be a potentiality of human nature which automatically erupts when the lid is off." If we view delinquency as mere action, then surely the kinds of acts that are usually considered delinquent—for instance, taking things from others, attacking others, and striking and cutting up things—are part of the human nature in that they are potentials inherent in our biopsychic endowment. One need only observe infants to realize that humans like other primates are *naturally* capable of the naive performance of deeds that are commonly considered criminal. Though such natural behavior does not "erupt automatically when the lid is off," it obviously will appear with considerable regularity. Thus, if Cohen and Short mean delinquency as action, then their critique of social control theories loses much of its initial plausibility, since naive behavior that is commonly considered delinquent is indeed a potentiality of human nature.

However, delinquency is only epiphenomenally action. As I have stressed throughout, delinquency is essentially infraction. It is rule-breaking behavior performed by juveniles aware that they are violating the law and of the nature of their deed, and made permissible by the neutralization of infractious elements. Thus, Cohen and Short are fundamentally right when they insist that social control theory is incomplete unless it provides an impetus by which the potential for delinquency may be realized.

The impetus for the commission of crime in classical criminology was will. Such a conception has many shortcomings. However, we must be sure that in rejecting it we do not do so for reasons that are now perhaps obsolete. The original positivist rejection of will was clearly metaphysical, as was its classical defense. It was rejected because, according to Lombroso, Ferri, and others, no such thing as will existed. Man did not make decisions. Like chemical particles, though unbeknownst to him, man was thrust from one situation to another. Nowadays, our rejection of a conception of will would lie on fundamentally different grounds. We would immediately and perhaps condescendingly grant that no such thing as will exists. Will, like any other concept—say, decision making—is an abstraction by which we hopefully make sense of concrete happenings. We no longer care whether will exists; only whether it enlightens.

A conception of will has not been terribly enlightening and thus it is not utilized. Why has it been unenlightening, and what can be done to render it useful? A conception of will is unenlightening primarily because it has traditionally served to beg the question. What we obviously wish to know is how, why, or when the will to crime becomes activated. Once we recognize that the reason for rejecting a formulation attributing crime to will is that it begs the question, the shortcoming may be ameliorated. We may refrain from begging the question by looking behind the conception of a will to crime, and inquire into the conditions that possibly activate it. However, in probing the conditions that possibly activate a will to crime, we need not search for the whole explanation of crime. The search is much more limited since we merely wish to know what activates the will to crime when juveniles have *already* been unbound from the compunction to behave lawfully. Thus, the conception of will need not carry the whole burden of explanation, as it came close to doing in classical criminology. Instead, it may represent the missing element needed in social control theory by which the potential for delinquency implicit in drift can be realized.

Two conditions that serve to activate the will or decision to commit an infraction may be suggested. Neither is operative outside the permissive context of drift. One condition serves to activate the will to crime on mundane occasions, the other serves the same function in more extraordinary situations. The first may provide the impetus for the repetition of old infractions, the second the thrust for new, previously unexperienced misdeeds. Both provide the nerve required of children for the commission of infraction. The first may be termed *preparation;* the second, *desperation.*

Will and Preparation

The will to repeat old infractions requires nothing very dramatic or forceful. Once the bind of law has been neutralized and the delinquent put in drift, all that seems necessary to provide the will to repeat old infractions is preparation.

By preparation I mean learning through experience that something that is commonly regarded as an infraction *can* be done, and thus, through the extension implicit in childish equivocation and the moral holiday implicit in drift, *may* be done. Such learning is truly a discovery, for until they have experimented with the forbidden, children are largely unaware that infraction is feasible behavior.[3] The childish equivocation may work both ways. If one may not do something, he cannot do it—not until he has tried it. Part of the learning connected with preparation consists of merely going through the actual motions implicit in one or another infraction; but only part, since if that were all that was involved we could also learn that such behavior is unfeasible. Thus, there is more to preparation than simply having previously experienced the commission of an offense. For the will to crime to be activated, the offender must learn that the offense is, after all, something that is relatively easy to do. How is that learned?

The overall feasibility of infraction involves both a moral and technical element. We need only focus on the technical element, since the moral feasibility of infraction is precisely what is taken care of by neutralization and subsequent drift. Neutralization makes the offense morally feasible since it serves to obliterate, or put out of mind, the dereliction implicit in it.

Technical feasibility, too, may be conceived in two senses. Each is implicit in the meaning of infraction. An infraction is an action taken in violation of a rule for which there is an expectation of legitimate counteraction. Though I have stressed the sense in which delinquency is best viewed as infraction, I have not intended to suggest that infraction is devoid of substantive action. That would obviously be an impossible state of affairs. Infraction includes action but transcends it. Infraction pertains to the interplay of *action* and *counteraction* on a moral grid. Consequently, technical feasibility consists of the learned capacity to manage the action, or *behavioral component* of delinquency, on the one hand, and the counteraction, or *apprehensive component,* on the other.

Preparation and the Behavioral Component

The will to repeat an old offense is not likely to be activated if in the past the performer has consistently flopped on his face or otherwise disappointed the behavioral expectations of others. Few persons—clowns and fools are among them—like to engage in activities they do badly. Delinquency like most things can be done badly, and thus those who do it very badly may choose not to—unless they are compelled, committed, or otherwise coerced. As Richard Cloward has persuasively argued, failure in the legitimate order does not guarantee success on the less legitimate side.[4] Delinquents, given as they are to sounding and bravado, are not likely to be supportive of persistently clumsy or inept execution of offense. We may suspect that at least a few juveniles have been deterred from specific delinquencies—though not necessarily from the subculture—by barbed reminders that they were hardly impressive the last time they tried that offense.

However, the level of proficiency implicit in the behavioral standards of subcultural delinquency may be easily romanticized, and correspondingly the difficulties of meeting these standards easily exaggerated. For a few drifting juveniles, the will to repeat old infractions may remain inactive because they anticipate the embarrassment and derogation stemming from their lack of proficiency. But whether the behavioral standards of subcultural delinquency are capable of deterring large numbers of drifting boys depends on how rigorous and demanding they are. Though we cannot be certain, we may reason that the behavioral standards of subcultural delinquency are high enough to discourage the will to crime among a few inept boys, but not so high as to deter most boys in drift. The delinquent enterprise and the behavior implicit in it is not after all a profession; little expertise or specialization is apparent.[5] Like its respectable counterpart—the school system —it seems tolerant of mediocre performance, which is merely to say that such performance elicits ordinary run-of-the-mill sounding, but no more. Moreover, the basic proficiencies required in delinquent action (others are involved in managing the apprehensive component) are not very different from those involved in common boyhood activity. Any reasonably good athlete can, *behaviorally*, be an excellent delinquent. All that seems necessary is some modicum of strength, dexterity, speed, agility, and cunning. Most boys probably possess or may easily develop the behavioral proficiencies implicit in delinquency. Thus, all but a few, once in drift, find the repetition of old infractions behaviorally feasible. They are able to manage the rudimentary skills involved in, say, shoplifting, burglary, or strongarm, and are in that measure prepared to reenter the infraction. In that sense, they possess the will to crime.

Preparation and the Apprehensive Component

A lack of the minimal behavioral proficiencies serves to discourage a few boys; their will to crime remains inactive despite the lifting of moral restraint implicit in neutralization. Another handful, probably larger, do not muster the will to crime because they are unable to manage the apprehensive component of infraction. They are in that sense unprepared for crime despite being in drift. They are, in the language of their companions, chicken, and in the language of classical criminology, deterred.

Some boys cannot manage the apprehensive component of infraction. However, that does not mean that infractions are necessarily rationally calculated or planned; merely that the will to crime is encouraged when the predictable counteracting efforts of official authority are not seen as so menacing and thwarting that the potential offender is immobilized, and the culmination of drift forestalled. If drifting boys are too scared, too apprehensive, about repeating an old offense because they recall the fear they experienced last time, the will to crime is obviously discouraged. Thus, it is important that they be prepared by past experiences to manage and in large measure discount the apprehensiveness they normally feel upon entering the infraction. This may be accomplished in a number of ways.

Subcultural beliefs regarding the technical incompetence of officials (discussed in Chapter 4) provide a substantial measure of relief from apprehensiveness. Subcultural delinquents are not overly impressed with the apprehensive capacities of law-enforcement officials. They are more likely to be impressed with their own potency, and thus believe that the chances of capture are slight. Indeed, their ability to evade apprehension and frustrate the official system is perhaps the most important source of subcultural delusions of potency. The objective intricacies and the inherent difficulties of the apprehensive process allow the delinquent to impute subjective incompetence to official agents, and to be misled regarding his own capacities. The exigencies of the apprehensive process, which make capture relatively unlikely except in the most serious of crimes, are reified and imputed to the protagonists in the criminal drama. Police are incompetent and they are potent. The theory implicit in these beliefs is erroneous but tenable. It is erroneous because the most convincing explanation of the frequent evasion of apprehension is found in the sheer objective difficulty of the apprehensive enterprise, not in the superior skill or potency of subcultural delinquents. However, their theory is tenable and even plausible because, like many defective theories, it more or less jibes with the observed facts. Delinquents in fact do evade apprehension the vast majority of the time. Since the theory of police incompetence and delinquent potency is tenable, it may be of service. It serves as a major means of discounting apprehensiveness, and thus is part of the preparation underlying the will to crime.

A second way of managing the apprehensiveness connected with infraction is to discount the *consequences* of effective counteraction. Even if official agents should succeed in apprehending the juvenile offender, appropriate experience may yield the knowledge that sanctions are frequently indecisive, trivial, or not forthcoming. One may learn that law may be violated many times with a measure of relative impunity. Subcultural delinquents typically learn that there is a large quota of chances—each solemnly described as the final one—before the weighty sanction of incarceration is forthcoming. This is not to say that lesser sanctions, like probation, are welcomed; rather, that the increments of sanction are typically small. The official system normally begins by responding to the delinquent with light sanctions and slowly and gradually proceeds to weightier punishments. The official system proceeds gradually partially because it is committed to an ideology of child welfare, but mainly because the system responds to the sequence and severity of delinquent infraction. The delinquent sequence is itself normally a process of gradual development, beginning with minor offenses and proceeding slowly to more serious crimes.[6] Consequently, the increments of sanction are sufficiently slight and administered gradually enough so that each appears not much worse than the one preceding it. The subcultural delinquent is inadvertently assisted in discounting the apprehensiveness connected with infraction by being gradually hardened to the more severe forms of sanction. Consequently, the apprehensiveness may be managed. The will to repeat a crime may be activated.

Will and Desperation

The will to enter new infractions is not easily activated. Like all new experiences, but especially those that are fraught with objective danger, new infractions are encountered with considerable trepidation. Thus, drift is not likely to culminate in new or previously unexperienced infraction unless the will to crime receives massive activation. Such activation may be provided by a feeling of desperation.

Desperation may have many sources but one looms largest among subcultural delinquents because it simultaneously serves to neutralize the legal bind and to elicit the situation of company. Thus, one variety of neutralization—the mood of fatalism—is of central importance because of the variety of functions it may simultaneously serve. The mood of fatalism neutralizes the legal bind since it renders subcultural adherents irresponsible: it elicits or is itself provoked by the situation of company because it exacerbates the feeling of dependency on peers who unlike others can be presumed to experience similar moods: and, finally, it provides a sense of desperation.

Why may the mood of fatalism provide a sense of desperation? The mood of fatalism, it will be recalled, refers to the experience of seeing one's self as effect. It is elicited by being "pushed around" and yields the feeling that one's self exercises no control over the circumstances surrounding it and the destiny awaiting it.

The fatalistic mood is not disconcerting for all persons, nor does it necessarily yield a sense of desperation. It is likely to have that effect only under certain conditions. Only persons who meet those conditions will experience desperation when caught in the mood of fatalism. As it happens, the major condition under which desperation flows from the fatalistic mood appears among subcultural delinquents.

The mood of fatalism is the negation of the sense of active mastery over one's environment. It is likely to culminate in a sense of desperation among persons who place profound stress on the capacity to control the surroundings. Such a stress is implicit in customary precepts that celebrate the virtues of manliness. A man is above all one who will not allow himself to be "pushed around." Thus, for subcultural delinquents to be "pushed around" and to be thrust into the mood of fatalism is tantamount to temporarily losing their prematurely and thus precariously gained manhood. In any setting in which manliness is stressed, celebrated, and regularly probed or sounded, the mood of fatalism will yield something approximating a sense of desperation. The subculture of delinquency is just such a setting. The customary precepts of subcultural delinquency which celebrate manliness conspire to increase the likelihood that desperation will flow from the fatalistic mood.

Subcultural delinquents experience desperation when caught in the mood of fatalism. Naturally enough, they seek to undo or cast away so unpleasant and undesired a state of being. They seek, in other words, to restore the mood of humanism in which the self is experienced as cause—the state in which man himself makes things happen. This understandable, even laudable, human desire leads to a remarkable and ironic turn of events. The restoration of the humanistic mood—and incidentally the restoration of the moral bind that is implicit in the *responsible* character of the humanistic mood—may be accomplished by the commission of infraction. The delinquent is rejoined to moral order by the commission of crime!

To restore the mood of humanism, the delinquent must make something happen. Not just anything will do. Just as he must be jolted into the fatalistic mood, so, too, he must be jolted back to humanistic mood. Some dramatic reassurance that he can still make things happen is necessary. Otherwise, the desperation of the fatalistic mood will linger. Mood is after all a deep and not a superficial human experience. The dramatic reassurance of the causal efficacy of self necessary for the restoration of the humanistic mood requires action, but not just any action. Many acts will not suffice since they hardly provide the thrilling jolt that simultaneously may cast out the self-doubt inherent in fatalism and restore the self-awareness inherent in humanism. Accustomed as he is to the rhythms and slights of sounding, the subcultural delinquent engages in an internal probing as he unwittingly searches about for deeds that may reconfirm his potency. Many acts are disqualified because, as his cronies would say if they were to sound him, "Shit, man, anybody can do that." Many acts, perhaps most, do not demonstrably make things happen. Only a few do. Prominent among acts that make things happen are those that are infractions. An infraction is among the few acts that immediately and demonstrably make things happen. Infraction properly and predictably invokes the criminal process. Thus, it may serve well as a symbol of restored potency.

Clearly, infractions do not exhaust the acts that may dramatically restore the humanistic mood. Any sort of outstanding performance or accomplishment might possibly perform a similar function. However, such things as athletic, scholastic, or heterosexual prowess, although they might restore the manly feeling of the humanistic mood, might also exacerbate the mood of fatalism since one may predictably suffer dismal failure as well as victorious success. Whatever other risks are entailed, the risk of deepening the fatalistic mood is absent in infraction. Delinquents may succeed in committing a theft or burglary by getting away with it, or they may fail and be apprehended; but in either case they have demonstrably made things happen. Even if they are caught, the mood of humanism may be restored. By committing an infraction, they have themselves made the counteraction of adult officials happen—no mean accomplishment. They have by their infraction put the criminal process in motion.

Because infraction is not the only means of resolving desperation, it does not necessarily follow every mood of fatalism. Other more uncertain methods can be and are used by subcultural delinquents, especially the exploitation and conquest of females. Moreover, the mood of fatalism may linger for long periods despite the desperation that accompanies it. But so, too, because infraction is a most certain and immediate way of being jolted back to the mood of humanism, it is frequently relied on. Reliance on infraction instead of other methods is additionally likely because of a coincidence: the same mood—fatalism—which yields desperation also elicits the situation of company. One function of the situation of company, it will be recalled, is to provide the context of mutual misconception, the context in which the subcultural delinquent comes closest to believing that he is committed to the precepts of a delinquent subculture.

The mood of fatalism neutralizes the bind to law, elicits the situation of company, and fosters a sense of desperation which in turn provides the will or thrust to commit a new infraction. Such desperation does not necessitate the commission of a previously unexperienced infraction. It merely provides the will or impetus for it. The repetition of an old infraction may do, but not as well unless it is undertaken under especially hazardous circumstances, since it may be defined and thus dismissed as "something anybody can do."

Desperation provides the will to commit new infractions; preparation, the will to repeat old infractions. Neither produces the infraction itself. Will, by definition, is something that may or may not be exercised. Will is an option. The will to crime may be activated by preparation or desperation. However, it may be discouraged, deterred, or diverted by countless contingencies. Though we may explore and perhaps specify the conditions that activate the will to crime, we cannot definitively state that a crime will be committed. Nevertheless, a conception of will may serve to represent the thrust, and thus enlighten the process by which the potential for crime implicit in drift is realized.

NOTES

1. Albert K. Cohen and James F. Short, "Research in Delinquent Subcultures," *The Journal of Social Issues,* Vol. XIV, 1958, p. 30.
2. *Ibid.*
3. For a somewhat similar discussion with regard to marihuana users, see Howard Becker, *Outsiders,* New York: Free Press of Glencoe, 1963.
4. Richard Cloward, "Illegitimate Means, Anomie and Deviant Behavior," *American Sociological Review,* April 1959, pp. 164–176.
5. Albert Cohen, *Delinquent Boys,* Glencoe: Free Press, 1955, Chap. 2.

6. Supporting evidence for a rough developmental sequence in delinquency proceeding from less serious to more serious offenses may be found in Ivan Nye and James Short, "Scaling Delinquent Behavior," *American Sociological Review*, June 1957, pp. 326–331; Clifford R. Shaw, *The Natural History of a Delinquent Career*, Chicago: University of Chicago Press, 1931; Clifford Shaw, Henry McKay, and James McDonall, *Brothers in Crime*, Chicago: University of Chicago Press, 1938.

Index